MERE
CHRISTIAN APOLOGETICS

MERE
CHRISTIAN APOLOGETICS

APOLOGETICS AND THE BIBLE IN SIMPLE TERMS

FOREWORD BY KENT HOVIND

JAMES STROUD

Copyright © 2017 James Stroud
All rights reserved.

ISBN: 1544288662
ISBN 13: 9781544288666

Acknowledgments

Special thanks to Tate publishing for doing this second edition (first published by Xulon Press).

Also, a sincere thank-you to Casey Luskin and the Discovery Institute (the think tank behind the Intelligent Design movement), who I have had the privilege to work with in several past events and who provided the foreword to my work *Philosophy of History: Naturalism and Religion* (as well as providing an abbreviated foreword here).

To William Lane Craig, with whom my wife and I had the honor of retracing many of the footsteps of the apostle Paul (through Italy, Greece, and Turkey in 2013).

To Ken Ham, with whom my wife and I had the opportunity to visit in 2010 and 2015.

To Kent Hovind, who I have kept contact with over the years and who has provided the foreword for this book as well as a DVD copy of his seminar (which will be included in books purchased from the Eureka Springs biblical history museum—www.NWABibleMuseum.org).

Many have asked me why in the world I would have allowed or wanted Dr. Hovind to provide the foreword for this book since he was found guilty of tax evasion (actually structuring not tax-evasion) and has been in prison for the last ten years (he was released the Summer of 2015). The short answer is that Dr. Hovind's work has not only influenced Creationism across the globe, his stance on academic freedom is more important now than ever, and for close to fifteen years, he offered to debate any atheistic or naturalistic professor showing his courage to take the Bible to the heart of the lion's den. But more than that, I find it quite appalling that Christian and non-Christian alike would expect Dr. Hovind to be without sin. Whether or not Dr. Hovind is guilty of tax fraud is somewhat a dubious point; he has now served his ten-year sentence. No one (other than Jesus of Nazareth) has ever been without sin, so why would I or anyone else expect Dr. Hovind or anyone else to be? I forgive him in the same way Christ forgives us if we ask in truth, and I pray that he too forgives us for perhaps turning our backs on him and judging him without knowing all the facts. (I for one stand with Dr. Hovind; see www.DrDino.com for more information)

By having both Luskin and Hovind provide the foreword, I hope that all sides can see that we share far more in common in the belief that naturalism is simply an illogical and outdated worldview than we do our differences concerning creationism. I pray this simple book will help us focus more on working together for a new generation in the name of Christ as opposed to bickering among one another. We have a common cause in Christ, and that should be enough for us all to rally behind.

I highly recommend one (if not all) of the following Bibles with commentary for better understanding of *Apologetics* and God's Word:

1. Morris, Henry M., and J. Gordon Henry. *The Henry Morris Study Bible: King James Version* (Green Forest, AR: Master Books, 2012).

2. Cabal, Ted, Chad Brand, Paul Copan, and James Porter Moreland. *The Apologetics Study Bible: Understand Why You Believe* (Nashville, TN: Holman Bible Publishers, 2007).

3. *Archaeological Study Bible: An Illustrated Walk through Biblical History and Culture: King James Version* (Grand Rapids, MI: Zondervan, 2010).

Contents

Foreword by Kent Hovind 9
Foreword by Casey Luskin 11
Preface 17
Introduction 23
1   Creationism and Intelligent Design 27
2   Darwinian Evolution versus Christian Creationism 41
3   The Historicity of Genesis as a Foundation 57
4   The Philosophy of Genesis as a Foundation 73
5   Can We Trust the Bible? 87
6   What about Religions Other Than Naturalism? 113
7   The Entire Biblical Story in a Nutshell 131
8   Main Events in Biblical History 151
Conclusion 159
Afterword 165
Appendix
Young Earth Creationism 169
Glossary 177
Bibliography 179
About the Author 183

Foreword by Kent Hovind

"There are many fine creationist organizations and speakers who are trying to stem the tide on humanism and evolutionism. It has been my privilege to meet many of them in the years I have been involved in creation ministry.

All creationists that I know are sincere and would not deliberately use false information but many differ on some issues. We all have points where we agree and points where we disagree with everyone but that should not hinder our Christian fellowship with each other." (Kent Hovind)

I was truly honored when I was asked to provide the Foreword for this book. After reading it I loved it and believe its concise nature will make it an important contribution to the field. I pray that this book will strengthen your faith in God's infallible word and will help you win souls to Christ. There are millions that need to hear this message.

The apostle Peter warned us (2 Pet. 3:3–8) that in the last days, there would be scoffers who are willingly ignorant of the creation, the flood, and the coming judgment.

Peter was right. They are here!

I commend James Stroud for his new book *Mere Christian Apologetics*. It adds a concise view of the accuracy of the Bible and provides a great deal of evidence to defend the faith against the scoffers.

I would like to personally thank James for this great work and for having me provide this short Foreword; I learned some really unique things in this very original work and am confident that you will as well.

—Dr. Kent Hovind
Founder of Creation Science Evangelism
www.2Peter3.com[1]

---

[1] Kent Hovind has been one of the most prominent voices for creationism in the late twentieth century. In the late 1980s, he began a full-time ministry of presenting the foundational truth of creation and the utter fallacy of evolution with a mission of strengthening the faith of believers and winning the lost to Christ. His award-winning, seven-part creation seminar continues to travel around the globe with translations in thirty-two languages (www.DrDino.com).

Foreword by Casey Luskin

"The court ruling for Dover schools banning intelligent design clearly has no relevance for Ohio. Ohio is not teaching intelligent design, making this a completely different issue. That was merely a ploy for Darwinists to keep students from learning about the evidence challenging Darwin's theory." (Casey Luskin)

I first met James Stroud in 2010, when he approached me regarding the work I had done with Discovery Institute defending academic freedom in public education. My second encounter with James was in 2012, when he hosted myself and Dr. John West at three universities, discussing modern scientific challenges to neo-Darwinian evolution. Evolutionary and atheistic scientists admit that we lack good explanations for key events in the history of the universe—the very events which Mr. Stroud discusses as being best explained by intelligent design (or creationism).

For example, in 2007, Harvard chemist George Whitesides was given the Priestley Medal, the highest award of the American

Chemical Society. During his acceptance speech, he offered a stark analysis of origin of life research, reprinted in the respected journal *Chemical and Engineering News*:

> The Origin of Life. This problem is one of the big ones in science. It begins to place life, and us, in the universe. Most chemists believe, as do I, that life emerged spontaneously from mixtures of molecules in the prebiotic Earth. How? I have no idea.[1]

Similar problems exist for the abrupt appearance of animal life, which has been dubbed as the Cambrian explosion. A 2009 paper in *BioEssays* concedes that "elucidating the materialistic basis of the Cambrian explosion has become more elusive, not less, the more we know about the event itself."[2]

In fact, the history of life is riddled with such "explosions," including an abrupt appearance of humans themselves. In 2004, the famed evolutionary biologist Ernst Mayr recognized the abrupt appearance of humans without a transition from the fossil record:

> The earliest fossils of *Homo*, *Homo rudolfensis* and *Homo erectus*, are separated from *Australopithecus* by a large, unbridged gap. How can we explain this seeming saltation? Not having any fossils that can serve as missing links, we have to fall back on the time-honored method of historical science, the construction of a historical narrative.[3]

---

1. George M. Whitesides, "Revolutions in Chemistry: Priestley Medalist George M. Whitesides' Address," *Chemical and Engineering News* 85 (March 26, 2007): 12–17.
2. Kevin J. Peterson, Michael R. Dietrich, and Mark A. McPeek, "MicroRNAs and metazoan macroevolution: insights into canalization, complexity, and the Cambrian explosion," *BioEssays* 31, no. 7 (2009): 736–747.
3. Ernst Mayr, *What Makes Biology Unique?* (Cambridge University Press, 2004), 198.

The same applies to the origin of human language and cognition. As MIT professor and linguist Noam Chomsky observes,

> Human language appears to be a unique phenomenon, without significant analogue in the animal world. If this is so, it is quite senseless to raise the problem of explaining the evolution of human language from more primitive systems of communication that appear at lower levels of intellectual capacity. ... There is no reason to suppose that the "gaps" are bridgeable.[4]

And finally, as for the origin of the universe itself, Stephen Hawking and Roger Penrose admit that "almost everyone now believes that the universe, and time itself, had a beginning at the big bang."[5] As Nobel Prize–winning physicist Charles Townes has stated, "Intelligent design, as one sees it from a scientific point of view, seems to be quite real. This is a very special universe: it's remarkable that it came out just this way. If the laws of physics weren't just the way they are, we couldn't be here at all."[6]

The point of this is that strictly materialistic/naturalistic explanations of nature are failing in many key areas. New approaches are necessary. In this regard, it is refreshing to see naturalistic Darwinism being tackled from the approach of philosophy of history, as Mr. Stroud has done here. It is also refreshing to see Mr. Stroud's compelling case that naturalism should not be a rule that is enforced upon academics to prevent

---

4 Noam Chomsky, *Language and Mind*, 3rd ed. (Cambridge: Cambridge University Press, 2006), 59.
5 Stephen Hawking and Roger Penrose, *The Nature of Space and Time* (Princeton, NJ: Princeton University Press, 1996), 20.
6 Bonnie Azab Powell, "'Explore as much as we can': Nobel Prize winner Charles Townes on evolution, intelligent design, and the meaning of life," *UC Berkeley News Center* (June 17, 2005), accessed March 14, 2012, http://www.berkeley.edu/news/media/releases/2005/06/17_townes.shtml.

them from following the evidence wherever it leads. Unfortunately, it seems that the more the evidence points away from naturalism, the more naturalists resort to strong-arm tactics to retain their cultural power.

Indeed, it's not hard to believe that ID proponents face persecution. After all, leading evolutionary scientists have admitted they would try to keep ID proponents out of the academy. In 2006, a professor of biochemistry and leading biochemistry textbook author at the University of Toronto, Laurence A. Moran, stated that a major public research university "should never have admitted" students who support ID and should "just flunk the lot of them and make room for smart students."[7] In 2011, Jerry Coyne, a leading evolutionary biologist at the University of Chicago, stated that "adherence to ID (which, after all, claims to be a nonreligious theory) should be absolute grounds for not hiring a science professor."[8] ID critics in some arenas have become so intolerant that in 2007, the Council of Europe, the leading European "human rights" organization, adopted a resolution calling ID a potential "threat to human rights!"[9]

These ID critics have every right to disagree with intelligent design. They should have every right to discuss and critique ID and publish their views. The problem is that they don't extend such rights to those who dissent from their position. But if there is no freedom to dissent, then there is no academic freedom. In

---

7   Casey Luskin, "Leading Biochemistry Textbook Author: Pro-ID undergraduates 'should never have [been] admitted,'" http://www.evolutionnews.org/2006/11/author_of_leading_biochemistry.html.
8   Michel Egnor, "Jerry Coyne: '…adherence to ID…should be absolute grounds for not hiring a science professor.',"http://www.evolutionnews.org/2011/03/jerry_coyne045001.html.
9   Council of Europe, "The Dangers of Creationism in Education," Last modified September 17, 2007, http://assembly.coe.int/main.asp?Link=/documents/workingdocs/doc07/edoc11375.htm.

this regard, the plight of ID proponents should be concerning not just to those who support intelligent design but also those who disagree with it. Academic freedom is a precious value that underlies our entire society. When non-naturalists lose academic freedom to pursue their ideas, everyone else loses as well. And this is true not just in the hard sciences but also in the social sciences like history and philosophy. In this regard, I applaud Mr. Stroud's argument that philosophy of history, like the natural sciences, should be "open" to the idea that naturalism is not necessarily true and therefore free to take the evidence wherever it leads.

—Casey Luskin
Intelligent Design Research Coordinator
Author and speaker at Discovery Institute
http://www.discovery.org/id/

Preface

> Follow the evidence, wherever it leads.
>
> —Socrates

Why another book? Because it is my opinion that while we can get a 300-page book on one Christian theological concept, we cannot get a simple book in less than 200 pages that adequately covers the Christian story in its entirety; one we can simply carry with us to reference for on-the-spot dialogue. It's also because several individuals requested a simpler read that was more concise and less technical than my previous work, *The Philosophy of History: Naturalism and Religion*, which was much more drawn out and very detailed. The following quote summarizes our current plight:

> Many high school seniors believe that Sodom and Gomorrah were husband and wife, while a majority of Americans cannot name one of the four Gospels. Jay Leno asked his Tonight Show audience one night to name one of Jesus' twelve apostles; they came up empty. One in ten Americans believes that Joan of Arc was Noah's wife, and only one-third knows that Jesus (not Billy Graham) preached the Sermon on the Mount. (*Washington Monthly*)

I believe this adequately sums up our current situation in the West and why we must revisit with believers and nonbelievers alike what it means to be a follower of Christ. In reference to C. S. Lewis's beautiful and still timely book *Mere Christianity* (which adequately peels back the layers to reveal Christ-ianity over church-ianity and all the various creeds and dogmas), I have titled this simple book *Mere Christian Apologetics* in a humble attempt to give a very simple and concise message of Christian theism that is virtually agreed to by all major branches of Christianity and that can be used simply to have a good understanding of why you are a Christian and what being a Christian means at a 101 level (so as to avoid being a statistic or someone who, like the quote above, is a Christian in name only, without understanding the basics of what it means).

I pray that this simple book can help you in better understanding the concepts of God, Christ, and the Bible. This book will hopefully serve all those who are interested in the concepts of truth as well as academic freedom to pursue that truth in all fields of academia. Christianity is becoming more and more hated by the secular world while ironically it is becoming more evidentially true than ever. Therefore, Christians should not be afraid of the "scarecrows" in the field of inquiry (placed there by the media and popular atheists) because I can assure you these straw men are quite harmless when one is prepared with the truth.

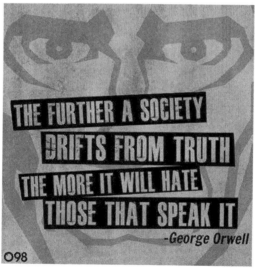

"The further a society drifts from truth the more it will hate those that speak it." (George Orwell)

I have had the privilege of working with the persecuted church for quite some time (www.persecution.com), and it is through their type of "underground seminary" that one can learn more in a month than in a year at the finest (and most expensive) seminaries in the world. The first century church was a persecuted church, one that knew that they had to trust in God every step of the way. A modern example is the church in China that in 1950 numbered approximately 750,000. These Christians were ruthlessly persecuted by the atheistic regime of Mao, but today they are estimated to be well over 100,000,000. On the flip side, the churches in Europe and Canada (and to a lesser degree, the United States) have plummeted. Some would accredit this to the "lesser developed" third-world countries still believing in superstitions while saying that the West is superior and knows better, but this is simply false. The concept of God and Christian theism (and biblical accuracy) is more highly respected now than it has ever been at the highest levels of science, history, and philosophy. Having finished my MA in ancient history and my BA in philosophy of religion, I have had the chance to debate the evidences for Christianity and biblical accuracy with many PhD atheists/agnostics, and they simply assert that they are right and we are wrong while conceding that the points brought up in favor of Christian Theism are accurate ones (see my much more detailed work *The Philosophy of History* for more intermediate information).

No, the reason for the West turning away from biblical Christianity is threefold:

- Biblical Christianity has been greatly watered down today to the point where one cannot tell the difference between a Christian and non-Christian outwardly or inwardly.

- Many Christians cannot adequately explain what Christianity is or why it is much more plausible than any other worldview.

- Christians have become in many ways like the church of Laodicea—lazy and more worried about political correctness and financial gain than they are with living out the Gospel. (Or as Francis Schaeffer described it: "Christians are more worried about 'personal peace and affluency' than on being Christian.")

Compare these three bullet points to the persecuted church. They may not be theologically savvy in some regards, but they live out their faith, even if it means their martyrdom. Unfortunately there is no denying that the West is post-Christian, and with that, we will see more laws against biblical Christianity, as well as more people leaving the faith for whatever is politically correct. At the same time, we will continue to see (as in Europe) more and more theologians and churches denying the Scriptures in favor of their own form of Christianity (which is not Christianity at all). If we (in the West) hope to live out our faith, we will have to think and prepare in many ways as the persecuted church does today. They know the Scriptures, and they know what it is like to be persecuted for their faith, but they also know how to live it out as the body and blood of Christ.

This is why I often use the example of the *Pilgrim Church*, so named after the book by the same name from E. H. Broadbent. Basically, all this means is that he looks at the small authentic and biblical Christian groups that throughout history have continued to carry the light of Christ's truth to its own generations, not the politically correct church or the state church, such as that of Constantine's day, but of the small church groups that met the needs of the people, regardless of class or social status, in sharing Christ and following His way and His way alone for attainting salvation and for meeting the needs of the poor and those in need. The Pilgrim Church can be the underground churches of Iran, China, and Russia today or the Lollards, Friars of Assisi, or St. Patricks of the past, or it can be you and me in a post-

Christian America that is becoming more and more hostile to anything Christian.

I highly recommend that you read *The Pilgrim Church* and get acquainted with just what the "white spaces between the lines" of church history does not always tell you. For our purposes, however, I am merely attempting to put together a simple book that you can carry with you for on-the-spot discussion of why we are Christians and how to tell others about it. In less than 200 pages, this is all too brief, but based on the current lack of biblical knowledge in the West today, I feel this is more worthwhile than any detailed breakdown of a certain aspect of biblical exegesis or philosophy. I pray that we will take the current sad state of the West in all seriousness, and if you are not a Christian, I challenge you to know what you believe. I have asked many atheists groups why they believed in naturalism (or atheism), and their answers are usually nonsensical, or they will be honest and just say, "Because I prefer to." If Christianity is true, then it should be the most important thing any of us think about, and it should permeate every facet of our lives. I truly pray that this simple and quite informal book with be beneficial to you. Please let me know if I can be of any assistance.

Please visit TheLollards.org or NWABibleMuseum.org to contact me or to do an online biblical and apologetics study (there's tons of free gifts at its conclusion). And please pray for me as well. I am far from perfect, and I too need prayer and help every day. We all must realize there is no shame at all in relying on Christ every day of our lives. Not relying on Christ is the real problem.

Please note that because I was challenged to keep this book less than 200 pages, I am only able to cover some areas very briefly; nonetheless, I pray that it sufficiently covers universally agreed messages by Christian theists, apologist, and skeptics alike in order to give you a quick reference tool for on-the-spot dialogue with an atheist, Christian, Muslim, Hindu, Buddhist, etc, on what it means to be a follower of Christ.

Also, in the back of the book is a glossary of terms to help better you familiarize with some of the common terms of philosophy.

> Remember the words I spoke to you: "No servant is greater than his master." If they persecuted me, they will persecute you also. If they obeyed my teaching, they will obey yours also.
>
> —John 15:20

Introduction

> A coherent worldview must be able to satisfactorily answer four questions: that of origin, meaning of life, morality, and destiny; while every major religion makes exclusive claims about truth, the Christian faith is unique in its ability to answer all four of these questions.
>
> —Ravi Zacharias

It is my utmost hope to place in your hands a small booklet that covers the major points of creationism through the Bible so that you may know and communicate to another person at a macro level why there must be a God, why Jesus Christ makes the most sense of the concept of God, how reliable the Bible is, and what the Bible says from cover to cover—all in less than 200 pages. The one advantage to this is that by my covering the basics at a macro level, this book would become equally usable for a nonbeliever searching for answers as well as for a believer from any type denomination. This is because I am explaining the basic tenants of each of these in an easy-to-understand way that virtually all believers or nonbelievers would agree with. We will not be doing a deep dive in eschatology or certain church doctrines. I will leave that for the reader to search out on their own if they would like. What this book will hopefully do is provide you with the same basic information that is 90 percent of what God, Jesus, the Bible, or the Good News is all about. So whether you are an Anabaptist, a Roman Catholic, an Anglican, a Protestant, an Eastern Orthodox, or a skeptic/agnostic, this book will give you the basics of what Christian biblical theism is in about 200 pages.

As mentioned in the preface, there is no denying that Europe, Canada, and now the United States is post-Christian. With that being said, it is important to review the rapidly dropping belief in God in the West:

Eurobarometer Poll 2010			
Country	"I believe there is a God"	"I believe there is some sort of spirit or life force"	"I don't believe there is any sort of spirit, God or life force"
Spain	59%	20%	19%
Lithuania	47%	37%	12%
Luxembourg	46%	22%	24%
Hungary	45%	34%	20%
Austria	44%	38%	12%
Germany	44%	25%	27%
Latvia	38%	48%	11%
United Kingdom	37%	33%	25%
Belgium	37%	31%	27%
Bulgaria	36%	43%	15%
Finland	33%	42%	22%
Slovenia	32%	36%	26%
Denmark	28%	47%	24%
Netherlands	28%	39%	30%
France	27%	27%	40%
Estonia	18%	50%	29%
Sweden	18%	45%	34%
Czech Republic	16%	44%	37%

Eurobarometer Poll 2010			
Country	"I believe there is a God"	"I believe there is some sort of spirit or life force"	"I don't believe there is any sort of spirit, God or life force"
Switzerland (EFTA, not EU)	44%	39%	11%
Iceland (EFTA, not EU)	31%	49%	18%
Norway (EFTA, not EU)	22%	44%	29%

The above poll (which has continued to drop since 2010) shows that belief in any God has been reduced across the board in Europe. In the 1990s, Americans were close to 90 percent Christian by most standards with less than 5 percent identifying as atheistic/agnostic, but today the belief in Christianity is approximately 73 percent, with 20 percent identifying themselves as having *no* religious affiliation. Surprisingly (as we will see), the atheist has no real reason "for" atheism (because it is a somewhat bankrupt worldview), so once the Christian theist is able to communicate the reasons for Christianity, as well as share the Good News of who exactly Christ is, we should expect to see the number of "authentic" believers increase. The problem is that today's Christian knows little to nothing about what or why they believe what they do. Even worse yet is, much like the late Francis Schaeffer predicted, many people realize atheism is not logical or defensible, so they have simply become apathetic and identified themselves as "none" or "nothing" when contemplating religion. Being apathetic simply means that whether Christian theism is true or not, they simply don't care. This is the fastest-growing religious affiliation and one of the most difficult to reach; nonetheless, Christians have a responsibility to reach all in the name of love.

- Christian apologetics is a field of Christian theology that aims to present a rational basis for the Christian faith, defend the faith against objections, and expose the perceived flaws of other worldviews.
- "But in your hearts revere Christ as Lord. Always be prepared to give an answer to everyone who asks you to give the reason for the hope that you have. But do this with gentleness and respect." (1 Pet. 3:15)

If we remember the above two points and adhere to them, then we should not see the type of statistics above or the quote below continuing to grow, keeping in mind the words of C. S. Lewis "that the greatest apologetic for the Christian is the life they live in witness to the world."

> Good News: 1/3 of Americans read their Bible at least once a week. Bad News: 54% can't name the authors of the Gospels. 63% don't know what a Gospel is. 58% can't name 5 of the 10 commandments. 10% think Joan of Arc was Noah's wife. (*New York Times*, 12/07/97)

1

Creationism and Intelligent Design

> As far as I can see, no strong arguments at all exist for naturalism but there are strong arguments against it. I therefore suggest that naturalism, like logical positivism, should be consigned to the scrap heap of philosophical history.
>
> —Alvin Plantinga, *Philosophia Christi*

Intelligent Design

While my book *The Philosophy of History* goes into much more detail on the subject, I am going to simply hit on the basics of each component and provide you with references and suggested sources of additional research at the end of this book, but from a starting point, it will be helpful to identify what we mean by *intelligent design* and *creationism* and why it matters to Christians.

The theory of intelligent design holds that certain features of the universe and of living things are best explained by an intelligent cause, not an undirected process such as natural selection. In a nutshell, a nonbeliever or any religion could be a supporter of ID (intelligent design) because it does not name the designer as a god or anything else; it simply looks at the evidence of naturalism (that everything can be explained by natural causation) and sees that since the chances of the universe coming into existence or life arising as the result of purely undirected material processes is effectively zero, an intelligent designer of some type makes the most sense. Design theorists favor the latter option and argue that our universe and living organisms look designed because they really were designed.

The author with Stephen C. Meyer, senior fellow of Discovery Institute and intelligent design advocate, author of the best seller *Signature in the Cell: DNA and the Evidence for Intelligent Design* and *Darwin's Doubt*.

The beautiful thing about ID is that it shows the weaknesses of naturalistic evolution (as we will look at later) but also allows us to communicate the evidence for a "creator" or "designer" to a secular audience or a skeptic, thus allowing us to effectively build a case for the fact that all arrows are increasingly pointing toward design as the cause of the universe as well as of life on earth. A good example of this is when I hosted Casey Luskin and John West from the Discovery Institute[1] at a three-university tour in 2012 on academic freedom and the strength of intelligent design as compared to Darwinian evolution. The crowd was very open to the information, with about 125 students and faculty showing up at the community college and 100 at the University of Arkansas, as well as the local atheists group and a few professors who wanted

---

1   I first hosted Luskin in 2010 at the University of Arkansas and then Luskin and John West at the University of Arkansas, John Brown University, and then Northwest Arkansas Community college on the strengths of intelligent design over that of Darwinian evolution.

us shut down (if they had the facts against ID and evidence for evolution, then why didn't they blow Luskin and Dr. West out of the water in front of a large crowd instead of going out of their way to shut it down?).

Some Christians (such as Ken Ham) object to ID because it does not specifically name the Christian God. Is this a valid argument? We must remember that anyone will tell you that one must believe that there is a god before they can believe in the Christian God. This is where ID makes perfect sense. It gives the philosophical and scientific facts behind the theory that there must be some type of designer without crossing the line in a secular setting and naming who or what the designer could be, thus adhering to what all of academia should in the old Socrates quote, "Follow the evidence where it leads." Agnostic astronomer Robert Jastrow came to this same ID conclusion in the 1970s when he wrote the book *God and the Astronomers*: "Consider the enormousness of the problem: Science has proved that the universe exploded into being at a certain moment. It asks: 'What cause produced this effect? Who or what put the matter or energy into the universe?' And science cannot answer these questions."[2]

Professor of law Phillip Johnson somewhat helped open the floodgates (along with Michael Denton in 1986) with his book *Evolution: A Theory in Crisis* that began a nonstop barrage of scientists, mathematicians, and philosophers publishing book after book on the impossibilities of Darwinian evolution. This was summed up beautifully in *Intelligent Design 101*:

> Intelligent Design really came to the forefront in the early 1990s among some scientists colleagues of mine who fell into various viewpoints. They agreed that there is fundamental evidence that lies behind the origin of life and the universe. This theory does not identify the mind. That is left to theologians. What the theory does say is that

---

2 Robert Jastrow, *God and the Astronomers*, 113–14.

science is capable of telling us that the universe and life bear detectable fingerprints of an intelligent designing agent. Intelligent design thus united into one movement people of many viewpoints who were once divided on side issues.[3]

Intelligent design theory thus allows us to connect to the next logical step within Christian theism, which is usually known as creationism. Creationism, for the most part, takes the scientific, philosophical, historic, and social sciences of intelligent design and then combines them with the Bible to make sense out of the world and universe we live in. While there are many different types of creationists who may differ on such topics as the age of the earth, all collectively agree on this:

intelligent design + the Bible = creationism

I have sadly seen too much debate between Christian groups over the details of the age of the earth, but I will agree with Ken Ham that we cannot compromise the Bible or Jesus of Nazareth with that of man's theories. For example, naturalism tells us a virgin birth is not possible, but this is a fundamental Christian belief, so I would caution any of us on relying too much on man's theories, which change every few years.

---

3 H. Wayne House, *Intelligent Design 101: Leading Experts Explain the Key Issues* (Grand Rapids, MI: Kregel Publications, 2008).

Answers in Genesis president and leading creationist, Ken Ham, with whom the author visited in 2010 and 2015.

Creationism

In a very broad nutshell, creationism is the belief that the earth and universe and the various kinds of animals and plants was created by God or some other supreme being. Those that hold the views of *creationism* are referred to as *creationists*. Within creationism in the Abrahamic religions, there are various ideas. In regard to those religions, one form of creationism holds that the earth is approximately six thousand to ten thousand years old and is referred to as young earth creationism. The other form of creationism is called old earth creationism and holds that the earth and universe are billions of years old. Creationist scientists believe that the first law and second law of thermodynamics argue against an eternal universe, and they also claim that these laws point to the universe being supernaturally created.

Dr. Norman Geisler stated that both young earthers and old earthers believe that God supernaturally, directly, and immediately produced every kind of animal and human as separate and genetically distinct forms of life. Dr. Norman Geisler also wrote that "both young- and old-earthers who are evangelical hold to the historicity of the Genesis account: They believe that Adam and Eve were literal people, the progenitors of the entire human race." Creation scientists show where the theory of evolution is in conflict with the evidence provided by the physical sciences and often cite secular scientific sources that agree with their own research.

Those who hold to young earth creationism point out that nearly every culture in the world has a creation story and a flood story. Many of these creation accounts and flood accounts have commonalities with the account given in the book of Genesis, which gives plausibility and historical scope to the Genesis account. The Institute for Creation Research has taken the position that the similarities of the creation accounts to the Genesis account demonstrate that the main points of the Genesis account has been preserved. Likewise, young earth creationists, particularly, show that there are strong similarities between the Genesis flood account and other world flood accounts. Also, there are remarkable similarities between Native American, Chinese, Persian, and other creation myths from around the world and the biblical account given in Genesis concerning creation. (On a side note, I prefer the term *creation history* over that of *creation science* since anything dealing with origins is history and not science per se, as my master's thesis in ancient history focused upon.)[4]

Creationism and Intelligent Design

Believers in the Abrahamic faiths who hold to creationism believe that the natural world has been designed by God. Recently, there have been more and more articles that are favorable to the intelligent design position in scientific journals, which traditionally have favored the macroevolutionary position. Believers in the Abrahamic faiths have points of agreement and disagreement with the intelligent design movement. They agree that the natural world has an intelligent cause and were designed as mentioned previously. However, as mentioned earlier, some advocates of creationism believe that the intelligent design

---

4 This thesis was published in the book *The Philosophy of History: Naturalism and Religion*.

movement divorces the Creator from creation by not explicitly stating that the cause of creation is a supernatural being and also failing to state explicitly who that supernatural being is.

There is considerable disagreement on whether or not intelligent design amounts to a form of creationism and, if so, where to place it in comparison to the other forms of creationism. This is due to the concept having many different definitions and proponents espousing different ideas. For example, one major proponent of intelligent design is young earth creationist Paul Nelson while Michael Behe, another major proponent, accepts common descent. William Dembski has stated unequivocally that intelligent design is not theistic evolution, and they should not be considered the same. Dembski has also written that intelligent design is the Logos in terms of information theory. He and others have given other definitions that do not include any specific theological references. Arguably, intelligent design can be summarized as the notion that at some point in the past, in some way, some entity (possibly God) created life or altered life or created the universe to be compatible with life. Creationism, on the other hand, believes that this creator is the God of the Bible, so if you believe that the God of the Bible is the intelligent designer who created the universe and everything in it as described in Genesis and throughout the Bible, then not only are you a supporter of ID, you are also a creationist.

Creationism and the Age of the Earth

I wasn't going to comment on this, but since a lot of people will inevitably ask, I thought I would very briefly touch on a few quick points, referencing heavily on the best summary I have seen in Wayne Grudem's book *Systematic Theology*. So what about the age of the universe or earth? I fall more into the Francis Schaeffer camp of agnosticism on the topic, I do, however, personally feel that historically and theologically speaking, the creation of all life only seems to be logical within a relatively young creation (perhaps 4,000–10,000 BC). The fact that the Bible says there was no death before sin and that through Adam sin entered into the world (see Rom. 5:12), we are left with either a young creation or a type of theodicy in which what we know as the past was created after Adam's sin since God transcends time. Thus, the ancient past came into existence after Adam's sin. Either are plausible, considering time is really beyond the realm of science just as the beginning of the universe is. Therefore, anything much more on the subject is simply speculative since no one was there.

I do not see any way to reconcile millions of years with humans emerging from ape-like ancestors—human death before sin, therefore there was no Adam, Eve, Noah, flood, fall, sin, temptation, etc., even though Jesus referenced them all—without losing the heart of Christianity, the Bible, and Christ himself. Moreover, in all my studies in ancient history, I do find it ironic that all of history seems to start around 3000 BC, with anything much before Gilgamesh (2700 BC) being simply assertions (we really only have good history as far back as Hammurabi around 1750 BC). The only reason we have begun assuming such long periods of time in the nineteenth and especially the twentieth century is because we assume Darwinism (and naturalism) is true and requires the long periods of time; thus, the assumption of these massive ages are very circular. The historians, as well as the Bible, seem to suggest (but not require) a relative recent creation. It is only modern science that necessitates billions of years because it presupposes that the Bible is false and naturalism is true, though it cannot defend either of these views. (Example: It was only a century ago that the proposed age of the universe was around 100 million years compared to today's 13.7 billion years.)

Therefore, I will simply encourage the reader to search this out on their own and just say that we must not sacrifice or placate the heart of the Christian message for the sake of man's ever-changing theories. In other words, if we say death was all around us before Adam or that Adam may not have really existed, then that automatically begs the question "Then what did Christ save us from exactly?" (See Rom. 5:12.) Moreover, if Adam was created an adult and not a baby, is it not possible the earth may appear old just as Adam appeared old? (And this is not "god of the gaps" reasoning any more than it would be to assume virgins don't give birth normally.) Again, this is far beyond the scope or purpose of this book, so I will simply end with a great quote on the subject from the theologian Wayne Grudem on the age issue:

> Although our conclusions are tentative, at this point in our understanding, Scriptures seem to be more easily understood to suggest a young earth view, while the observable facts of creationism seem increasingly to favor an old earth view. Both views are possible, but neither one is certain. And we must say very clearly that the age of the earth is a matter that is not directly taught in Scripture, but is something we can think about only by drawing more or less probable inferences from Scripture. Given this situation, it would seem best to admit that God may not allow us to find a clear solution to this question before Christ returns, and to encourage evangelical scientists and theologians who fall in both the young earth and old earth camps to begin to work together with much less arrogance, much more humility, and a much greater sense of cooperation in a common purpose.[5]

Even Atheists Recognize That Creation Is a Valid Necessity

Have you ever wondered where the universe came from? Why everything exists now as it is instead of just nothingness? Most people do not realize (or want to acknowledge) that the last one hundred years of scientific discoveries have pointed more to a designer than ever before. For many millennia, many thought of

---

5   Wayne Grudem, *Systematic Theology* (Downers Grove: IV Press, 1994), 307.

our vast universe as eternal and uncaused, but since the twentieth century, that has been universally abandoned in favor of a created universe. (I'm not sure if you have caught that or not, but what this means is all space, matter, and time itself began in the finite past or had a beginning point.) This cosmological discovery is now most often referred to as the big bang theory. The big bang is the cosmological model of the initial conditions and subsequent development of the universe that is supported by the most comprehensive and accurate explanations from current scientific evidence and observation. As used by cosmologists, the term *big bang* generally refers to the idea that the universe has expanded from a primordial hot and dense initial condition at some finite time in the past (currently estimated to have been approximately 13.7 billion years ago) and continues to expand to this day. This discovery alone verifies that the universe, space, matter, and time itself have an instantaneous beginning point. When they try and describe the big bang by naturalistic means, it simply does not make sense, and they have to assert and assume a great deal of things that the evidence does not support, whereas Genesis and the concept of God does explain and is less ad hoc and more plausible than a universe from nothing.

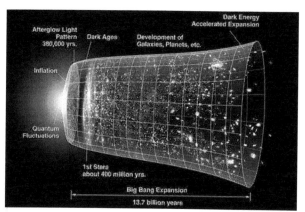

Standard big bang model that shows all of space/time/matter coming into being uncaused out of nothing at a finite point in the distant past, which begs the question, Why and how did it come into existence in the first place?

The implications of this finding are enormous, and unfortunately the ramifications are rarely spelled out to students. Even though it does not necessarily stipulate the God of the Bible, it does strongly support an intelligent designer of the cosmos (and moreover it does match well with the creation story of Genesis).

I think agnostic Robert Jastrow, who sat in the same chair as Edwin Hubble, sums it up best in his book *God and the Astronomers*: "This religious faith of the scientists is violated by the discovery that the world had a beginning under conditions in which the known laws of physics are not valid, and as a product of forces or circumstances we cannot discover. When that happens, the scientist has lost control."[6]

The discovery that the universe had a beginning was not met with pleasure. Many scientists rebelled against the notion because it implied a beginner. One scientist admitted, "The notion of a beginning is repugnant to me."[7] Yet the evidence was there. Jastrow puts his finger on the problem: "Many scientists have a 'religious' commitment to the assumption that everything has a natural, scientifically accessible and quantifiable explanation. Just when they were becoming confident in this assumption, seemingly explaining everything from the formation of stars to the formation of species, they ran into something which in principle cannot be explained scientifically: that first instant of creation, when the universe began as a singularity, a point inaccessible to investigation."[8]

Genesis gives us a historic record. We will simply leave it at this: both believer and nonbeliever recognize that the universe did have a first cause and a type of creation where not only space

---

6   Robert Jastrow. *God and the Astronomers*, 113–14.
7   Arthur Eddington. "The End of the World: From the Standpoint of Mathematical Physics," *Nature*, no. 127 (1931): 450.
8   Ibid.

and matter but also time itself came into existence through this first cause.

The Naturalist Opposing View Held in Textbooks as Superior to ID: Chance

Admitting design into science can only enrich the scientific enterprise. All the tried and true tools of science will remain intact. But design adds a new tool to the scientist's, philosopher's, and historian's explanatory tool chest. Moreover, design raises a whole new set of research questions. Once we know that something is designed, we will want to know how it was produced, to what extent the design is optimal, and what its purpose is. Note that we can detect design without knowing what something was designed for. There are rooms at the Smithsonian filled with objects that are obviously designed but whose specific purpose anthropologists do not understand, such as arrowheads.

So it is really up to you now. Is the brilliant theory of blind chance for everything sufficient? Or is the theory that there is an intelligent designer starting to make more sense? I have only touched on a few very basic philosophical points, but this should be enough, Lord willing, to at least establish that deism (that there is some type of creator or designer behind all of life) is more logically coherent than naturalism. In the next chapter, we will quickly review the basics of Darwinian naturalism, which is endorsed by secular academia as fact, to see how factual it really is because it is important for both the believer and nonbeliever to understand the arguments and what is at stake.

You should be able to answer these questions after reading this chapter:

1. What is the difference between intelligent design, creationism, and naturalism?
2. Why is naturalism less credible than creationism or intelligent design?

3. Can one believe in naturalistic evolution and Christian theism?
4. What is young earth creationism?

Here are the top 3 recommended readings for a greater understanding of this chapter:

1. *Biblical Creationism: What Each Book of the Bible Teaches about Creation and the Flood* by Henry Morris (2000)
2. *Understanding Intelligent Design: Everything You Need to Know in Plain Language* by William A. Dembski and Sean McDowell (2008)
3. *The Politically Incorrect Guide to Darwinism and Intelligent Design* by Jonathan Wells (2006)

2

Darwinian Evolution versus Christian Creationism

> Has anyone provided proof of God's inexistence? Not even close. Has quantum cosmology explained the emergence of the universe or why it is here? Not even close. Have our sciences explained why our universe seems to be fine-tuned to allow for the existence of life? Not even close. Are physicists and biologists willing to believe in anything so long as it is not religious thought? Close enough. Has secularism in the terrible 20th century been a force for good? Not even close, to being close. Does anything in the sciences or their philosophy justify the claim that religious belief is irrational? Not even in the ball park. Is scientific atheism a frivolous exercise in intellectual contempt? Dead on.
>
> —David Berlinski (agnostic)
> *The Devil's Delusion: Atheism and Its Scientific Pretensions*

Darwinian evolution is an incredibly slippery concept to define because it can mean so many different things. For the purpose of this book, we will go with the general definition held in school textbooks. Life somehow arose by chance following the big bang. Somehow nonlife gave rise to life, which then somehow slowly became all the different phylas we see today—the plants, animals, insects, etc.

The two premises on which the various theories of evolution are based are these:

1. This is the evolutionary formula for making a universe:
   Nothing + nothing = two elements + time = 92 natural elements + time = all physical laws and a completely structured universe of galaxies, systems, stars, planets, and moons orbiting in perfect balance and order.
2. This is the evolutionary formula for making life:
   Dirt/inorganic materials + water + time = living creatures.

Evolutionists theorize that the above two formulas can enable everything about us to make itself. (How ironic is it that this theory is held so viable today?) Contrast this with creationism or intelligent design theories that consider the possibility that an intelligent agent has to be the ultimate reality in which everything else can ultimately be traced back to (the uncaused cause); moreover, in Christian creationism, this intelligent agent is the Christian concept of God recorded in the Bible. Outlining these points and understanding them are of the utmost importance to anyone who is either Christian or Darwinist.

In a nutshell, the typical public school textbook will assert that for no reason, the universe (space/time/matter) came into existence about 13.7 billion years ago. Over the next several billion years, the universe continued to expand. Stars and planets began to form, and about 4.5 billion years ago, our earth formed in the picture-perfect area of the universe/galaxy (proper atmosphere, gravity, etc.), and when this all happened, there was still no life, so somehow nonliving materials became alive and slowly evolved into all life-forms, with humans being the only ones to develop consciousness and sentiency, and here we are today. **Now if this isn't absolute blind faith, I do not know what is.** I have asked many atheistic groups if this is what they believe, and (more or less) they agree that it is, and they feel that this is more plausible than God creating the universe and creating mankind in His image. It is literally dumbfounding that this is taught in most textbooks as fact.

Let us first define *science*:

Sci·ence (sī'əns) n.

1. The state of knowing.
   a. The observation, identification, description, experimental investigation, and theoretical explanation of phenomena.
   b. *Such activities restricted to a class of natural phenomena.*
   c. Such activities applied to an object of inquiry or study.
2. Methodological activity, discipline, or study: I've got packing a suitcase down to a science.
3. An activity that appears to require study and method: the science of purchasing.
4. Knowledge, especially that gained through experience.

Isn't it interesting how scientists say that they are open-minded, but by the very definition of *science*, they rule out any supernatural or metaphysical options (such activities restricted to a class of natural phenomena)? Science, at one point, simply meant "knowledge," then it grew to include the scientific method, and as you can see, now it encompasses several different definitions, in which the definition in letter B rules out anything other than natural phenomena. This seems to be self-refuting of the definition in number 1 (theoretical explanation of phenomena). Why is it that some of the most "free" nations in the developed world have the least freedom of inquiry when it comes to educational freedoms? As many of you have heard, there is an ever-increasing movement urging us to be able to simply follow the evidence where it leads regardless of the implications, but governmental agencies are restricting this very option, which is at the heart of science, freedom, and education. I would think anyone—theist, agnostic, or atheist—would welcome a true openness to all the facts and would support following the evidence where it leads, but this is becoming less and less so.

Charles Darwin himself said that all evidence should be given to the populace. (I truly think if Darwin were alive today, he would be a supporter of intelligent design theory.) When my great-grandparents were children, they were taught from a more theist approach in public schools, my grandparents from more of a deist approach, and my parents from more of an agnostic approach with a leaning toward theism. My generation saw a more straight agnostic approach, and now today's children are getting a more atheistic approach that does not allow them to take the evidence where it leads. This helps us see why public education is in such an abysmal state. This truly is not a warranted or scientific approach but an ideological one that unfortunately our elected officials and Christians as a whole have let happen without much of a fight.

Mere Christian Apologetics

As the 2008 documentary film *Expelled: No Intelligence Allowed* showed, our society has an ever-growing intolerance to anyone who challenges the naturalistic/Darwinist approach to explain origins. As I had mentioned earlier, we are living in a post-Christian America, but this is no reason for an inquiring mind, much less a Christian mind, to roll over and play dead. I am honestly dumbfounded by much of the way this has fallen apart and the inactivity that Christians are playing in it all.

We will first look at what evolution is and is not. One could break evolution into the following categories:

1. Cosmic evolution
2. Chemical evolution
3. Organic evolution
4. Macroevolution
5. Microevolution

Of these terms, only microevolution (change over time) has been verified. This term was never really controversial in the first place and existed well before Darwin. An example would be Eskimos having a higher fat content than someone who lives on the equator because they live in colder climates. Another example is the different kinds of cats, dogs, etc. There are some changes notable as the generations have gone on, but that is where it stops. We have big dogs and little dogs, but they are always dogs. This is an example of microevolution, which to my knowledge, no one contests.

The other theories are 100 percent speculative and must be followed with extreme faith. Organic/Macroevolution contends that at some point, everything can be traced back to a single cell that was created by complete chance, as mentioned above. (Modern evolutionary trees have slowly "evolved" to include four super groups—plants, parasites, fungi/all animals, and algae related.) This is related to the term we hear called *common descent*, which states that all living organisms on earth are descended from a common ancestor or ancestral gene pool. In layman's terms, this basically means that somehow beyond all probability, life came about from what is often called the primordial soup (chemical evolution) from the early earth, and then it somehow came to life and basically went through a series of drastic evolutionary changes/mutations, followed by natural selection to account for all the phyla, genera, species, etc., that we have today.

There are an incalculable number of problems with this theory. First of all, it cannot be tested; therefore, it sets itself up as unfalsifiable. We cannot test origin science, so cosmic, chemical, and organic evolutions are 100 percent conjectured. We do not see any of these changes happening at present, and we cannot duplicate any of these experiments, so we are left with conjecturing and theorizing, but there is no data available for us to have any real confidence in these speculations. We also do not have any reason to believe that macroevolution is plausible (Example: a non-dog eventually becoming a dog or a bacteria becoming a non-bacteria). We have never seen this happen (because once again, it would take millions of years), there should be a plethora of transitional intermediary fossils found, but there are not. Moreover, the metamorphic changes required are grossly neglected by the vast majority of supporters to this idea.

In a nutshell, what this means is that we never see any type of transition of one animal evolving into another (evolutionists say it takes millions of years, so we wouldn't notice it), so in theory, *if* evolution was true, then we should see a fossil like a cow, then another one a little less like a cow and another one less and less and less and each one progressing toward, let's say, a whale (since the cow-to-whale evolution model is one that the evolutionists say is their strongest). But the facts are that we have none of these. We have a few fossils that may look like a cow, then one that looks like a seal and one that looks like a whale, so the evolutionists "infer" that this means that Darwinian evolution is true. The problem is that math tells us there would have to be *at least* fifty thousand transitions between the cow and whale, so there should be a plethora of fossils confirming this. Even if there were (which there are not), it would still be an "interpretation" of the fossils. This is no joke (I encourage you to research it yourself), and this is one of the evolutionist's strongest evidences?

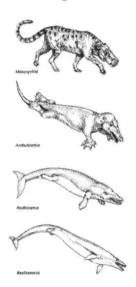

The supposed cow-to-whale evolution model of "magical change over time." Mathematicians have calculated that at least fifty thousand intermediate changes would be needed if this model were true (not 4).

With this type of lack of evidence, coupled with the fact that our oldest fossils of beavers, dogs, trees, insects, and even animals like the platypus all look exactly like they do today, with the exception of minor changes and larger overall size, we begin to see why more and more people are abandoning Darwinism for ID/creationism. The cow-to-whale transition, as mentioned above, is supposed to be one of the stronger evidences in favor of evolution, but mathematician David Berlinski has calculated at least fifty thousand metamorphic changes would be required to go from the cow to the whale. We do not see any evidence for this today. We do not see any evidence for this in the fossil record. Nor would the fossils even be able to give us a great picture because they are untestable themselves. (In fact, we are not able to prove anything by looking at a seal fossil and a walrus fossil that one "changed" into the other.) Once again, it is speculation that everyone is entitled to make, but this is a relatively weak theory when all that has been proven since well before Darwin is that we see variations within genus. We have all types of different people, but we do not have half-ape, half-man creatures. Nor do we have any reason to think there ever were such creatures. Think about it. We should not only have at least some species/genera of ape-men still alive, we should also have a ton of fossils showing these intermediary changes.

Instead we see a history of more than one hundred years of frauds and fakes trying to find just one single ape-man for Darwinists to get behind. I encourage you to research these on your own, but just to name a few of the famous fakes of history that still exist in some textbooks, there's the Piltdown Man, Nebraska Man, Peking Man, Lucy, and the list goes on. While I was attending the University of Arkansas, I took a class in 2001 titled Biological Anthropology, which focused primarily on human evolution. The professor could not answer questions surrounding these frauds or what was supposedly guiding these changes. Nor would he acknowledge that these interpretations were dependent on the philosophy of science and not empirical science. Ironically, many of the "missing links" that were mapped out during the class were changed a few years later because new fossil discoveries proved their evolutionary tree wrong. It also caused scientists yet again to acknowledge the complexity of attempting to force together evidence that does not exist. It is hard for me to believe when I see top scientists pick up four or five fossils and say that they prove something such as the cow-to-whale evolution or when they find a single tooth (such as in the case of the Nebraska Man) and say that tooth proves that humans evolved from apes. (The tooth ended up being that of a pig.) The list continues to grow, with usually at least two to three headlines per year on the cover of *Science*, *Time*, or *National Geographic* exclaiming, "Missing Link Found For Sure This Time!"

What about creationist science? While there is no way to do this subject justice in such a small book, I can give a quick example of creationist and PhD scientist Dr. Jack Cuozzo and his research on the Neanderthal in *Buried Alive: The Startling Truth about Neanderthal Man*. In his research, Dr. Cuozzo has personally studied, x-rayed, and analyzed many of the original Neanderthal bones and came to the conclusions that the longer/thicker brow ridges as well as skull development (completely absent from the youth) were due to great ages (well over 100 years old). Dr. Cuozzo sees a commonality here with the rapidly diminishing life expectancies after the Flood of Noah, when the Bible says mankind still enjoyed longer than normal life expectancy. Therefore Dr. Cuozzo came to the conclusions through his meticulous research that Neanderthal was really not that much different than you or I. While Dr. Cuozzo was quite revolutionary in postulating such theories, more and more scientists (both Christian and non-Christian) are sharing many of Dr. Cuozzo's conclusions. Genetic evidence by secular scientists suggest that Neanderthals contributed to the DNA of modern humans, which is exactly what Dr. Cuozzo concluded twenty years ago when he took the Bible as his starting point of understanding.

Similarly, for half a century, Anthony Flew was the world's most famous intellectual atheist. Then in 2004, he made a shocking announcement: "God must exist." In a headline-making reversal, Flew then held that the universe must be the work of an intelligent designer. In an interview for Philosophia Christi, he added, "It now seems to me that the findings of more than fifty years of DNA research have provided materials for a new and enormously powerful argument to design."[1]

More and more scientists are agreeing with Antony Flew. The world appears designed because it is designed. They argue that the design in the world is just as real as the design in a computer, a car, or a sports stadium. These scientists have also observed another surprising thing: the hard empirical evidence for Darwinism is in fact very, very limited. Darwin's mechanism of natural selection acting on random variations can account for small-scale changes in living forms: variations in species themselves. But neither Darwin's mechanism nor any other purely natural mechanism explains how insects and birds came to exist in the first place. The theory is supposed to explain such large-scale adaptations, but it doesn't, and there has not ever

---

[1] Gary Habermas and Antony Flew, "My Pilgrimage from Atheism to Theism: A Discussion between Antony Flew and Gary Habermas," *Philosophia Christi* 6 (2004): 197–211.

been *one single* point of evidence other than pure speculation and guessing, so I am utterly dumbfounded why, after 150 years from the release of Darwin's book, this theory is still taken seriously. (This is part of the reason that debating the ideas have decreased while state censorship has increased. If you cannot prove ID or creationism wrong, then just make it illegal to teach and get the media on your side, then two plus two might equal five, regardless of whether it really does or not.)

While we could dive into book after book on the theory of evolution, enough has been said to establish a solid base that evolution requires at least as much faith as the hypothesis of a supernatural creator does. However, I am by no means using a type of "God of the gaps" theory that many will claim.[2] I simply continue to reveal the hard-core facts to both hypothesize and challenge you to do the same because none of the basic premises I am saying here are disagreed upon even by those who are Darwinists themselves. I am only using the most basic of facts without going into the minute details. I merely seek to review the topics discussed on a macro, easily accessible approach to give both laymen and experts a reason to sit back and contemplate. What we can establish is that evolution does now qualify as an ideology and philosophy more than it does as a credible interpretation of the facts. So while we can all agree with change over time, also known as microevolution, any other type of evolution past this point is speculative at best. When a group accepts all the definitions of evolution discussed earlier as fact and begins incorporating these in all their various outlooks, this becomes an ideology that many now call Neo-Darwinism.

---

2   Again, for a much more intermediate (and more formal) breakdown, please see *The Philosophy of History*, which was based off of my master's thesis; this current work is just a toe-in-the-water account as I have had many ask me for a simpler and more informal read.

I had the privilege of having dinner with Dr. Jonathan Wells at the Discovery Institute in Seattle in the summer of 2009. Dr. Wells has PhDs from both Yale and Berkeley Universities, with one being in cell and molecular biology. It is interesting that he too confirms the complete fraud of Darwinism. Like me, he is dumbfounded why so many adhere to a theory that has developed into an ideology. In his book *Icon of Evolution*, he goes through a list of repeated hoaxes and outright lies that have been (and still are) used to support evolution in public school textbooks, magazines, museums, and so on for the last century. In regard to human evolution, he states with reference to Henry Gee, chief science writer for *Nature*: the conventional picture of human evolution as lines of ancestry and descent is a "completely human invention created after the fact, shaped to accord with human prejudices."[3] Putting it even more bluntly, Gee concludes, to take a line of fossils and claim that they represent a lineage is not a scientific hypothesis that can be tested but an assertion that carries the same validity as a bedtime story—amusing, perhaps even instructive, but not scientific.

---

3 Henry Gee, *The Accidental Species: Misunderstandings of Human Evolution* (University of Chicago Press, 2015), 102.

When asked further about this type of information being given to the general public Dr. Wells states,

> The general public is rarely informed of the deep-seated uncertainty about human origins that is reflected in these statements by scientific experts. Instead, we are simply fed the latest version of somebody's theory, without being told that paleoanthropologists themselves cannot agree over it. And typically, the theory is illustrated with fanciful drawings of cave men, or human actors wearing heavy makeup. Whether the ultimate icon is presented in the form of a picture or a narrative, it is old-fashioned materialistic philosophy disguised as modern empirical science.[4]

What about "Theistic Evolution?"

I attended a seminar in 2011 at Westminster Seminary in Philadelphia where philosopher Dr. Jay Richards, cosmologist Guillermo Gonzalez, biologist Paul Nelson, and many theologians reviewed the irony of how many Christians are attempting to reconcile Christian theism with Darwinian evolutionism. Interesting to note is (as I eluded to above) that attempting to

---

4   Jonathan Wells, *Icons of Evolution: Science and Myth* (Washington DC: Regnery Publishing, 2001), 225.

link a creator god with a naturalistic/no-god hypothesis is not only impossible and self-contradictory, it is a logical fallacy (like saying you believe that circles are square or that you are a married bachelor). By their very definitions, they cannot be linked; one is either a theist or an atheist, but you cannot be both. So how can we possibly attempt to use a strictly unguided naturalistic process to describe how God guided the process? We have already discussed why evolution is not a very probable explanation for how life developed from a nontheistic view; moreover, it is absolutely an illogical concept for one to claim a belief in bridging Darwinism with theism to get theistic evolution. Most supporters of this view that I have encountered quickly abandon the view when we begin to discuss it simply because they did not have a full grasp of what it implied and how it contradicted not only probability and science as we know it but also Christian theology. So if someone tells us that they believe in "theistic evolution," we should push them to explain what they mean by these terms (most likely it will either not be theistic or it will not be evolution).

Was Adam and Eve highly intelligent primates? Of all the questions that can be raised about the theory of evolution, none is more vital than whether humans evolved from nonhuman animals. In naturalistic evolutionism, human beings were not created with a dignity transcending all other animals but instead are simply a particularly intelligent primate. The biblical teaching is that the human race has fallen from an original innocence and that our tendencies to violence, greed, lust, deceit, and selfishness are in some sense unnatural for us. This teaching is at direct odds with the notion that the human race evolved from a similar primate species and that our unethical tendencies are actually part of our evolutionary history (a.k.a. survival of the fittest). For these reasons and more, I would not be a Darwinist even if I were not a theist. There are simply too many missing links within the theory of evolution to believe it to be true. This is part of the reason that more and more atheists are abandoning naturalism holistically, even though they may still remain nontheists. For example, atheistic philosopher Thomas Nagel recently wrote *Mind and Cosmos: Why the Materialist Neo-Darwinian Conception of Nature Is Almost Certainly False*. Though Nagel does not embrace Christianity, he acknowledges that he cannot refute the Christians' arguments (such as Alvin Plantinga's). Nor can he defend Neo-Darwinism. It is a good sign that the atheists are starting to realize that not only is naturalism implausible but that Christian theism makes a lot of sense. Not surprisingly, many atheists have attacked their former hero Nagel with the publication of this book. Apparently, one is supposed to continue to support the religions of naturalism/atheism regardless of whether there is any warrant for doing so or not.

While this is only skimming the surface of the subject, in the next chapter, we will review if the creation account itself portrayed in the Bible can better cover the naturalist theory of chance by testing them both for

- logical consistency,
- empirical adequacies, and
- experiential relevance.

Please keep in mind that I am not discussing anything in this book that is overly complicated so that everyone can understand and expound on the subject in order to point others to the plausibility of God and the Bible (and the irrationality of naturalism).

You should be able to answer these questions after reading this chapter:

1. What are the different types of evolution?
2. Which types of evolution have been observed?
3. Can one believe in Darwinian evolution and Christianity?
4. Why is evolution a weak theory?

5. How would you answer someone who asked, "Why do you believe in creationism over naturalism?"

Here are the top 3 recommended readings for a greater understanding of this chapter:

1. *God and Evolution* by Jay W. Richards (2010)
2. *Darwin on Trial* by Phillip E. Johnson (2010)
3. *The Lie: Evolution* (Revised and Expanded) by Ken Ham (2012)

3

The Historicity of Genesis as a Foundation

> The first eleven chapters of the Bible have been relegated by many to the category of myths, not real history. What makes it more intense is that in the ranks of those Christians who have not compromised the historicity of Genesis are many scientists with doctoral degrees from the modern education system.
>
> —Andrew Snelling,
> *Genesis: Real, Reliable, Historical*

Genesis: A Book of Beginnings

I believe the book of Genesis not only provides the overall strongest understanding of the ultimate reality/intelligence we collectively call God but that it also reveals much more than simply the book of beginnings for the Hebrew nation. I believe it can be traced back to the very beginnings of mankind itself. If my hypothesis is true, then we should be able to see a very similar Genesis 1–11 type of story throughout various cultures and writings of the ancient world. We should also see that while modern science and cosmological theories change yearly, there remains nothing to disprove the account of creation given by the Genesis account. Lastly, we should be able to establish some type of validity in the historicity portrayed by the ancient Genesis account. If these three measures are successfully fulfilled, then we have a cumulative case argument for my hypothesis of the Genesis account being accurate and applying to not just the

Hebrew nation but all of mankind. This will help us to better bridge the gap between the intelligent designer and Christianity.

Details concerning the Writings of Genesis

While both Jewish and early Christian tradition consistently states that the whole Torah (including Genesis) was authored by Moses (as with the Talmud, Mishnah, and most Old and New Testament references), there is limited information on how it is so, especially with Genesis predating him. Assuming that Moses was responsible for the book of Genesis as we now see it, there seems to only be three possible explanations for how he attained these stories and recorded them in what became known as the Torah. Moses either received all the Genesis accounts by direct revelation from God, he received them by oral traditions passed down from the beginnings of time, or he took actual written records of the past and collected them into a final form known to us today as Genesis. For the direction of this book, I will make a case for a combination of all three points, with an emphasis on the last point.

Israel was not alone in formulating explanations for the world's beginnings. All the great civilizations of the ancient Near East had literature that described how the universe began. Surprisingly the most ancient records and artifacts of the oldest civilization in the world also seem to give plausibility to the Genesis record. China is often considered a civilization of ancestral worship, with Taoism, Buddhism, and Confucianism, yet if we look at the times before all these other worldviews, we find a very different religious atmosphere. We find evidence of an ancient people who served only one god called Shang-ti (Lacouperie). It is supposed that the Chinese originally migrated from a site in Mesopotamia because of various Babylon-Assyrian similarities in arts, sciences, and government. The approximate dates of their origin at 2500 BC is surprisingly close to the strict dating of the great event described in Genesis as the Tower of Babel.[1] Though all views concerning the past do vary, there are reasons to believe that the Chinese written language bears a testimony to prehistory, which matches with the Genesis account. Not to go into too much Chinese character detail, but we see at the radical base of the Chinese language many peculiar finds that seem to lend credence to the Genesis account one thousand years before Moses was born. While the symbols within the language are not conclusive, we do see, for example, that the Chinese character for *create* is comprised of three symbols: speak, dust, life (God speaks man into existence from the dirt). We also see *forbidden* comprised of two trees and God (tree of good/evil). *Boat* is comprised of three symbols: vessel, eight, and people (Noah's ark + eight total people saved):

A sample of the Chinese symbol for boat, giving us a possible clue to its ancient origin, found within the Genesis narrative. (www.AnswersInGenesis.org)

While this is only three quick examples, there are many more within the language, as well as within the most ancient manuscripts of China (*Shu ching: Book of History*), dating back

---

1 C. H. Kang and Ethel R. Nelson, *The Discovery of Genesis: How the Truths of Genesis Were Found Hidden in the Chinese Language* (St. Louis: Concordia Pub. House, 1979), 162–85.

to the supposed time of Genesis's Noah.[2] Within this book are records of the first three dynasties of Hsia, Shang, and Chou and several of their predecessors embracing the period from about 2450 to 721 BC. Also of note is the earliest account of religious worship by Emperor Shun in 2230 BC, where he sacrifices to this one god known as Shang-ti. But can this Shang-ti be identified as the same God of Genesis? The following quote is from the recitation script of the emperor who served as a type of high priest:

> Of old in the beginning, there was the great chaos, without form and dark. The five elements had not begun to revolve, nor the sun and the moon shine. In the midst thereof there existed neither forms nor sound. Thou, O spiritual Sovereign camest forth in thy presidency, and first didst divide the grosser parts from the purer. Thou madest heaven; Thou madest earth; Thou madest man. All things with their reproducing power got their being.[3]

This recitation extolling ShangTi as Creator does sound quite similar to that of the Genesis account. "In the beginning God created the heavens and the earth. The earth was without form and void, and darkness was upon the face of the deep…" (Genesis 1)

When we look at the various creation accounts that either predated Genesis or would have been separated from it, we seem

---

2   Ethel R. Nelson, Richard E. Broadberry, and Ginger Tong Chock, *God's Promise to the Chinese* (Dunlap, TN: Read Books Publisher, 1997).

3   The classical concept of five elements is different from the modern concept, which comes from Buddhism. In the classical concept, the five elements were wood, fire, earth, metal, and water. These were seen as underlying many phenomena, both physical and conceptual/spiritual, and many things were classified according to their supposed underlying element. The five planets were one outworking of the five elements in classical Chinese thinking.

to find reoccurring accounts from various traditions. When we look at the Enuma Elish, Sumerian Eridu Genesis, the writings of Lao-tzu, Egyptian myths, Hinduism's Brahman, etc., we see a very similar Genesis-like pattern:

> Before time, and throughout time, there has been a self-existing being, eternal, infinite, complete, omnipresent... Outside this being, before the beginning, there was nothing.[4]
>
> I am the creator of all things that exist...that came forth my mouth. Heaven and earth did not exist, nor had been created the herbs of the ground nor the creeping things. I raised them out of the primeval abyss from a state of non-being.[5]

While much more could be said for example on the Ebla tablets (that predate the Babylonian account by almost six hundred years and again are very familiar to the Genesis account) and other legends, the value of these various quotes lies in the fact that this knowledge of, in other words, "a Genesis-like" creation existed quite independently of the biblical Genesis amid cultures that were and are quite separated from Judaism or come much later in Christianity but offer support to the Bible's creation account.

Creation Account versus Cosmology

If this creation account is authentic, then we must assume it is also accurate for all times. With the opening lines of Genesis, we see what most would call creation ex nihilo or creation out of nothing. The book of Genesis stands alone in the accounting for the actual creation of the basic space/matter/time continuum, which constitutes our physical universe. While other creation

---

4   Laozi, Gia-Fu Feng, and Jane English, *Tao Te Ching* (New York: Vintage Books, 1972), 13.
5   This is my paraphrasing of Wallace Budge's literal translation in *The Gods of the Egyptians*, vol. 1 (Dover, New York, 1969), 308–313.

stories discuss creation from other things, it is only the Bible that discusses a literal creation from nothing. Genesis 1:1 is unique from every other system of cosmogony, which starts with eternal matter or energy in some form. Only the book of Genesis even attempts to account for the ultimate origin of matter, space, and time. What is amazing is that while many within the realms of science held to an eternal universe for hundreds of years, discoveries in the twentieth century have indeed confirmed what appears to be creation ex nihilo in the finite past, most often referred to in cosmology as the big bang. What is remarkable about this is that even atheistic scientists have concluded beyond reasonable doubt that all of space/time/matter began in an unexplained instant. As mentioned earlier, agnostic astronomer Robert Jastrow, who held the same seat as Edwin Hubble, seems to confirm the accuracy of the Genesis account in the following comment in his book *God and the Astronomers*:

> Now we see how the astronomical evidence supports the biblical view of the origin of the world….the essential elements in the astronomical and biblical accounts of Genesis are the same. Consider the enormousness of the problem: Science has proved that the universe exploded into being at a certain moment. It asks: 'What cause produced this effect? Who or what put the matter or energy into the universe?' And science cannot answer these questions.[6]

Likewise, Genesis explains the origin of man as being in the likeness of God himself. What we find is that of all created beings, science recognizes man alone as being a sentient being. Agnostic astronomer Paul Davies commented in an interview that while it is logical for man to evolve the abilities to run, climb trees, hunt, and so on, it does not seem necessary for him to develop a consciousness by mere chance, to ponder the

---

6   Robert Jastrow, *God and the Astronomers*, 3–4.

stars or how they were created or how atoms are held together or why anything at all exists instead of nothing. Genesis 1:27 seems to stand alone in its description of why mankind might possess these types of inner workings and ponderings. These type of skills are certainly not required in the hunter-gatherer sense, but the Genesis account does seem to make logical sense as an explanation. While we are just beginning to scratch the surface of research, we can begin to see a strong cumulative case argument forming for the Genesis account possibly being applicable not just to the Hebrew nation, but to all nations of the world, thus confirming the accuracy of Genesis as a foundational study in all cultures to our understanding (however limited) of God.

As with the Creation accounts, the global flood narrative in Genesis 6–9 can be shown to be more realistic and less mythological than one might think when we begin to look at the surrounding facts. Dr. Duane Gish has recorded *270 similar flood legends* from around the world matching that of the Genesis flood while explorer Graham Hancock has recorded over 500.[7] The Flood is told of by the Greeks, Hindus, Chinese, Mexicans, Algonquians, Hawaiians, and Sioux Native Americans, just to name a few. The Chinese record a man named Fuhi and his wife, three sons, and three daughters escaping a great flood and being the only people alive on earth. A flood story in Hawaii records that Nu-u and his family escaped a global flood by building a great canoe and filling it with animals. Only he and his family were left alive.

While these stories, as well as the Gilgamesh story, are different in parts of their narrative, the overall themes are shared in all of them, which seems to be far more than mere coincidence. Moreover, there is geological evidence to support a worldwide flood. Partial skeletons of recent animals are found

---

7   Don Landis. *The Genius of Ancient Man: Evolution's Nightmare* (Green Forest, AR: Master Books, 2012), 75–76.

in deep fissures in several parts of the world. There are fossils found in almost every mountaintop (including Mount Everest). Sedimentary rock layers, which are formed underwater are found in all parts of the world, and we find whale skeletons and other marine life in the Sahara desert. The Flood seems to be a possible explanation of these, if not the best explanation altogether. Again this is not "forcing" the evidence to fit a preconceived view, but in the realm of historic studies, all we can do is look at the past and make assumptions based on the evidences we have today. Why are there hundreds of very similar flood legends found throughout cultures and history? Why are there fossils found across all of the continents? Maybe an actual flood (as described in the Bible) is the best explanation.

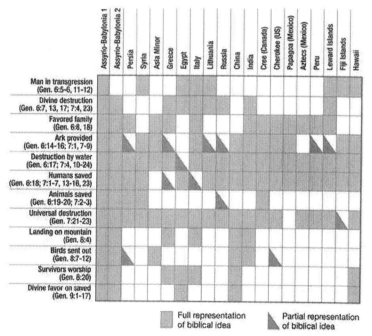

A sample of the matching accounts of a Noah-type global flood recorded in almost every culture across the world. (www.AnswersInGenesis.org)

The Historicity of the Genesis

All tests so far (while not conclusive) have seemed to point out that the book of Genesis could indeed be a book of beginnings for all of mankind, but is it complete in its historicity and explanatory scope? Even higher critics have often admitted that the tenth chapter of Genesis (concerning mankind's genealogy) is a remarkably accurate historical document. There is no comparable catalog of ancient nations available from any other source. It is unparalleled in its antiquity and comprehensiveness. William F. Albright, who was known as the world's leading authority on the archaeology of the Near East (and himself did not believe in the infallibility of the Bible), said concerning the Table of Nations in Genesis 10: "It stands absolutely alone in ancient literature, without a remote parallel, even among the Greeks, where we find the closest approach to a distribution of peoples in genealogical framework...The Table of Nations remains an astonishingly accurate document."[8]

Here we find the one link between the historic nations of antiquity and the prehistoric times pre-Noah and the antediluvians recorded in Genesis. While many other than Dr. Albright have studied the Table of Nations, I stumbled across a book by Bill Cooper of the United Kingdom called *After the Flood*, where he provides genealogical sketches, documented manuscripts, and much more to trace the sons of Noah to the Chinese, the Aryan race of India, the European cultures, etc., from this Table of Nations:

> The test I devised was a simple one. If the names of the individuals, families, peoples, and tribes listed in the Table of Nations were genuine, then those names should appear also in the records of other nations in the Middle East. While I would have been quite content if I could have vindicated

---

8   Henry Morris, *The Genesis Record*, 245.

40% of these; today I can say that the names so far vindicated in the Table of Nations make up over 99% of the list, and I shall make no further comment on that other than to say that no other ancient historical document of purely human authorship could be expected to yield such a level of corroboration as that![9]

While a historian could still say these are not 100 percent certain, they would likewise have to admit that as of today, they have yet to be refuted for their historical and genealogical accuracies.

When we read Genesis 11:1–9, we see an explanation for why the nations were scattered into different groups as well as human language in the event known as the Tower of Babel. There is considerable evidence now that the world did indeed have a single language at one time. The Sumerian literature alludes to this several times, as does many other cultures across the globe. Linguists also find this theory helpful in categorizing languages. Sanskrit was the classical language of India and today is considered the primary bridge between Hebrew and other Semitic languages and the Greek/Phoenician and Latin of Western civilization. Gothic, Celtic, and Persian/Farsi languages also are now known as the Indo-European family of languages, but the similarities are not confined to this family. Wayne Jackson stated that the ancient languages of Assyria and Egypt had much in common with those of the Maya and Inca peoples of the Americas. Language scholars were rapidly concluding that all languages had a common root in the 1970s.[10] Even secular scholars now admit that all languages did come from one common root (though they may or may not believe in the Tower of Babel story). From here (Genesis 12), we see the Genesis account unfolding with the calling of a

---

9   Bill Cooper, *After the Flood*, 12.
10 Wayne Jackson, "Languages of the Bible," https://www.christiancourier.com/articles/200-languages-of-the-bible.

particular nation and a particular man, Abram (later to be known as Abraham), to lead his people toward the land of Canaan, and thus the story of the Bible unfolds with Abraham, Isaac, Jacob, and the twelve sons/tribes of the eventual land known today as Israel.

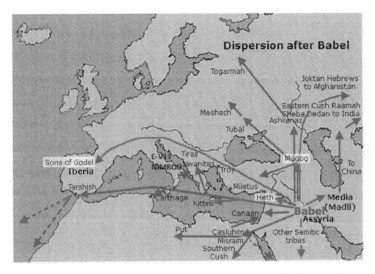

So what does this all mean? While I only touched on a fraction of corroborative sources that show a multiplicity of supporting factors for the Genesis account's scope going far beyond that of the Hebrew nation, I do believe we have seen enough support to form what philosophers call a cumulative case argument for the accuracy levels of Genesis 1–11 going far beyond mere coincidence could allow; allowing us to form the conclusion that the Genesis book of beginnings is not merely for the beginning of the Hebrew nation but for all of mankind. Nothing has been discovered to disprove the Bible in centuries of trying to find evidences against it. Instead, we find with every new discovery or archaeological find, the biblical narrative grows in support and continues to stand up to the test of time and form the exegetical foundations for the rest of the Bible so that creation, sin, death, sacrificial systems, murder, flood, languages, and repopulation of the earth from the Arafat/Sumerian area all make sense and have supporting explanatory scope when we take the Genesis account as accurate and not fictional, thus giving even more credence to the Christian concept of God.

For the scope of this book, being limited to less than 200 pages in total length, I have had to greatly reduce the amount of information that I would like to dive into. I have provided extra sources to reference at the end of each chapter if one is so inclined to further their research, but I would highly recommend the Bible itself to be read again afresh. Not only is the Bible written by at least forty authors and not only does it span from 2000 BC to the fifth century BC (Old/Hebrew Testament) to the AD 1st century (New Testament), but is considered by historians like myself as the most accurate historic literature in ancient history in both quality and quantity. (Some historians may not agree with the Bible or its inspiration, of course, but none that I know of will argue that it is better attested historically, quality- and quantity-wise, than any other ancient writings that we know of, and this alone makes it a worthy read by all seeking to better understand the past.)

To summarize the main points of this chapter, let's remember the following bullets:

- Cosmological origins endorsed by secular sciences, such as the big bang theory, have concluded what the Genesis account has always stated, that space, matter, and time itself all began in an instance in the finite past (Gen. 1:1).

- The origin of life on earth has always been a mystery that secular sciences have concluded somehow arose from rocks and other inorganic materials, whereas the Genesis account shows that this origin is from a designer (which keeps with the law of biogenesis that life only comes from other life).

- The creation of animal and human consciousness (sentiency) is not some isolated miracle but a reflection of the underlying structure of reality. While the secular scientists attribute this to chance, the Genesis account of humans being created in the image of God with special attributes, including consciousness and sentiency, does seem more applicable than mere unexplainable chance.

- The account of a "fall" (from God's grace) and the introduction of sacrifice recorded in Genesis makes sense of the human condition or predicament of being separated from this being (God) and explains why almost every religious system has some type of sacrificial atonement base to it (and why religion exists in the first place for all ancient civilizations). Moreover, the idea makes more sense when the Christian theist links it to Jesus of Nazareth (discussed later).

- The idea of a global flood is recorded in almost every culture (270+ different accounts). Most of these legends, which record that only a few righteous survived along with animals on a boat to repopulate the earth, fit in with the Genesis recording of the flood and, though somewhat fantastical, explains such phenomena as the vast amount of fossils that were buried all over the world. (Remember, before Charles Lyell and Charles Darwin's principles of long ages took hold 150 years ago, most geologists held to a global flood as a credible explanation of the facts.)

- The idea of Noah's ark resting around the Arafat region also matches well with the first recorded civilizations arising in the nearby Sumerian and Mesopotamian regions and spreading out from there across Asia, Africa, and Europe.

- The Tower of Babel account in Genesis explains how/why languages were mixed and civilizations spread out from the Arafat/Sumerian region. Atheists acknowledge that the records of language and civilizations seem to arise almost instantly without any evolutionary development. The Genesis account would explain why this is.

- The Table of Nations recorded in Genesis 10 provides a verifiable genealogy of the kingdoms arising since the global flood and the sons of Noah, which has been verified by critics as remarkably accurate and without comparison in any ancient genealogy and has so far not been proven false in any way. The fact is that its statements can be sufficiently tested. Genesis 10 of the Bible has been found incredibly accurate, resulting partly from linguistic studies, partly from archaeology, and, more recently still, from the findings of physical anthropologists who are to this day recovering important clues to lines of migration in ancient historic times.

- We then see the calling of Abraham as the beginnings of the Hebrew nation, in which archaeology has done nothing but help support and confirm, which of course makes sense if the Genesis accounts are accurate.

While these are only a few basic facts surrounding what we know of our world in comparison to the Genesis account, it does seem to continually make sense of why we see the first recorded languages, civilizations, histories, etc., arising no earlier than around 4000 BC. It also explains why they exploded at about the same time with no evolutionary system of writing or speech patterns where people are grunting or slowly learning to communicate in written form. So once again, we have firm evidence that it is no coincidence that trying to explain our world through "chance/evolution" does not make sense, but if we think for a moment that the Genesis account and the Bible may be accurate as history and archaeology continually are proving, we find that the story of history, philosophy, linguistics, anthropology, etc., all do make sense. Therefore, the Genesis account does not only serve as the foundation of the Bible, which Jesus quoted from repeatedly, it also has the best explanatory scope of any competing hypothesis in understanding our origins. And please keep in mind that I do not really consider myself a young earth creationist in the Ken Ham sense, where I am dogmatically saying that creation happened at 4004 BC at midnight.

As I have written in *The Philosophy of History*, which contains data that was compiled during my master's thesis in ancient history from a secular university, whether the universe began 13.7 billion years ago or 10,000 years ago, it did not come from nothing, and this is why the Genesis account is so remarkable. All I am saying is that from history, all we know is what I have stated above, and this does fit in nicely with a recent creation, but I am agnostic on exactly when creation happened. The late Henry Morris said in *The Genesis Flood* that though he leaned more toward the 4000 BC time frame, he was open to a time line from 10,000–4000 BC due to various dating and genealogies (ex: the Septuagint (Greek Old Testament) dates creation closer to 5500 BC and many theologians throughout history have agreed to the 5500 creation date over that of the 4004 one). So once again, my point is simply that old earth or young earth, we are on the same side and agree with much more than we disagree. Theologically and historically, a recent creation seems to make the most sense based on what we see but (as I break down in *The Philosophy of History*) one can take an old earth or universe, and the secularists are still left trying to explain why anything at all exists, how the universe came into being, how life arose, and how civilization (language, writing, arts, religion, etc.), as well as morality and sentiency, arose. These questions all need to be answered, and Genesis (old or young) provides plausible and coherent answers.

You should be able to answer these questions after reading this chapter:

1. Does Genesis (the first book of the Bible) provide good evidence for the creation of the universe, life, and civilization that modern science has confirmed?
2. How many flood legends like that of Noah's ark have been discovered?
3. Is the Tower of Babel a possibly explanation of the spreading out of civilization after the Flood? (Explain.)
4. Does the Table of Nations provide extra evidence for the genealogy after the flood?
5. Has any biblical archaeology discovery ever discredited anything from the Genesis account?

Here are my top 3 recommended readings for a greater understanding this chapter:

1. *The Genesis Record: A Scientific and Devotional Commentary on the Book of Beginnings* by Henry M. Morris (2009)
2. *After the Flood: The Early Post-flood History of Europe Traced Back to Noah* by Bill Cooper (1995)
3. *The Stones Cry Out: What Archaeology Reveals about the Truth of the Bible* by Randall Price (1997)

4

The Philosophy of Genesis as a Foundation

> For since the creation of the world His invisible attributes, His eternal power and divine nature, have been clearly seen, being understood through what has been made, so that they are without excuse.
>
> —Romans 1:20 (NIV)

The Argument from Purpose

If God does not exist, then life is ultimately meaningless. As William Lane Craig points out,

> If your life is doomed to end in death, then ultimately it does not matter how you live. If there is no God, then man and the universe are doomed. Like prisoners condemned to death, we await our unavoidable execution. There is no God, and there is no immortality. And what is the consequence of this? It means that life itself is absurd. It means that the life we have is without ultimate significance, value, or purpose.[1]

In other words, there is no point to anything. So what if you're rich or if you are good or bad? Nothing matters, and in the end, there is no ultimate difference whether you existed or not. This fact should at least make a person think and reflect on life in general.

---

1 William Lane Craig, http://www.reasonablefaith.org/the-absurdity-of-life-without-god.

On the other hand, if God does exist, then not only does life have meaning and hope, there is also the possibility of coming to know God and his love personally. Therefore, I'm inclined to agree with the French mathematical genius Blasé Pascal (and the argument of Pascal's Wager) that even if the evidence for or against God is equal, the rational thing to do would be to believe in God's existence. That is to say, if the evidence is balanced, then why would someone prefer to bet on death and despair over hope and significance? Therefore, as Craig put it, "I'm inclined to speak of the presumption of theism: we ought to presume that God exists unless we have some good reason to think that atheism is true."[2]

At this point, the only negation I have ever heard of this is, "Yeah! Life and existence are totally pointless! Who cares?" They are fighting a losing battle, in other words. At this point, we should at least be able to encourage someone to reflect on the importance and ramifications of the totality of purpose and meaning. (Even issues such as gay rights, transgenderism, environmental extremism, etc., there is no purpose to any of these things if there is no God. We are all here by accident, and the entire human race will eventually die in the heat death of this part of the galaxy, so how could any of it matter outside of God?)

Introduction to Philosophical Reasoning

Philosophy is the rational investigation of the truths and principles of being, knowledge, or conduct. Just to give you a brief introduction of how a deductive argument works (before we jump right into it), I want to give you a very basic example to help you wrap your mind around it. Here is a basic logical inference:

1. Jon is taller than Scott.
2. Scott is taller than Jane.

---

2 Ibid.

3. Therefore, Jon is taller than Jane.

In this simple example, if premise 1 and 2 are correct, then 3 must logically follow. It is irrelevant how tall the persons in question are. *If* Jon is taller than Scott and Scott taller than Jane, it is a logical necessity that Jon is taller than Jane. Arguments like this can either be deductive or inductive. An inductive argument makes it *probable* that the conclusion is true if the premises are true while a deductive argument *guarantees* that the conclusion is true if the premises are true. The argument must be sound, not question-begging, and all the premises leading to the conclusion must be more plausible than their denials. For an argument to be certain, we must have certainty in the premises leading up to its conclusion, whether it is two premises, as above, or one hundred. If someone could provide evidences that Jon was on stilts when he was measured against Scott's height in the above example, then premise 1 could be false (if it was shown without the stilts that Scott was indeed taller), and therefore my entire argument would collapse. But so long as a statement is more plausible than its negation, we should believe it rather than its negation.

The Cosmological Argument

The cosmological argument is an argument for the existence of a first cause (or instead, an uncaused cause) to the universe and, by extension, is often used as an argument for the existence of an "unconditioned" or "supreme" being, usually then identified as God. It is traditionally known as an argument from universal causation, an argument from first cause, the causal argument, or the argument from existence.

This allows us to formulate the three following points:

1. Whatever begins to exist has a cause.
2. The universe began to exist.
3. Therefore the universe has a cause.

Someone might say, "So what?" But the point is inescapable. If the universe began to exist, then it has a cause. Since space, matter, and time itself began at this point (usually called the big bang), the cause must be greater or beyond space, matter, and time or, in other words, spaceless, matterless, and timeless. In other words, this is a very powerful cause, and it chooses to create (since there is no reason to believe that the universe must have come into existence, it simply could never have happened); therefore, it is personal. So what we have is a personal creator that sounds a lot like what people usually mean by God. I will just provide you with a few easily assessable examples that overwhelmingly point to God and away from atheism so that you can become familiar with how such reasoning works. Remember, if the premises are true, then the conclusion must follow:

1. Whatever begins to exist has a cause.
2. The universe began to exist.
3. Therefore the universe has a cause.
4. This cause must be beyond space, time, and matter.
5. This cause must be personal (since it chooses to create).
6. This cause is best explained by being a personal God.

The Teleological Argument

The next area we'll quickly look at is the fine-tuning of the universe. If the universe began to exist from a point in the past, then it is highly unlikely that everything came together the way it needs for us to even be able to exist, by chance it would seem. Did we simply get lucky as the naturalists would have us believe? Why is the universe fine-tuned, and what exactly does this mean? This apparent fine-tuning of the universe is cited by many as evidence for the existence of God or some form of intelligence capable of manipulating (or designing) the basic physics that govern the universe.

The fine-tuned universe is the idea that the conditions that allow life in the universe can only occur when certain universal cosmological constants lie within a very narrow range, so that if any of several fundamental constants were only slightly different, the universe would be unlikely to be conducive to the establishment and development of matter, astronomical structures, elemental diversity, or life as it is presently understood (in layman's terms what this means is that it is practically impossible that we just hit the lottery of lotteries in the fact that our place in the universe is literally perfectly made for us to even be able to exist). One of the greatest philosophers alive today, Alvin Plantinga, argues that random chance applied to a single and sole universe only raises the question as to why this universe could be so lucky as to have precise conditions that support life at some place (the earth) and time (within millions of years of the present).

The degree of fine-tuning is difficult to imagine. Dr. Hugh Ross gives an example of the least fine-tuned of the cosmological constants in his book *The Creator and the Cosmos*, which is reproduced here:

> One part in 10^{37} is such an incredibly sensitive balance that it is hard to visualize. The following analogy might help: Cover the entire North American continent in dimes all the way up to the moon, a height of about 239,000 miles. Next, pile dimes from here to the moon on a billion other continents the same size as North America. Paint one dime red and mix it into the billions of piles of dimes. Blindfold a friend and ask him to pick out one dime. The odds that he will pick the red dime are one in 10^{37}. The nature of the universe reveals that a purely naturalistic cause for the universe is extremely unlikely and, therefore, illogical. One cannot say that a miraculous naturalistic event is a scientific explanation since miracles are only possible when an immensely powerful Being intervenes to cause them. When a model does not work, scientists must be willing to give up their model for a model that fits the facts better. In this case, the supernatural

design model fits the data much better than the naturalistic random chance model.³

Naturalistic Darwinists normally choose the default explanation that the entire fine-tuning is simply due to chance. Moreover many naturalists now have begun to cling to the multiverse hypothesis in a desperate attempt to say *if* there were millions of other universes, then the fine-tuning impossibilities decrease. This literally is the atheist saying, "Well, what if there were millions of other universes? That would make it easier to understand why our place in the galaxy is in the perfect place for us to be able to exist." Keep in mind that there is literally zero evidence that there are any other universes other than our own, which shows the great lengths naturalists and our public school systems have to go to skew the evidence in avoiding any type of God/designer in explaining fine-tuning.

Just to give you a simple comparison of what the majority of people mean by chance, let me explain. We use chance every day in some way. For example, if we hear on the weather forecast that there is a 90 percent chance of rain versus a 10 percent chance of no rain, there is a fairly high probability that it will rain. Science likewise calculates such subjective statistics to determine whether something might or might not occur. In day-to-day life, we can say that an event that has only one chance of occurrence in 10^8 (100 million) is considered an impossibility. To break it down, if you picked up a rock and dropped it 100 million times and each time it fell to the ground, we have established that gravity is very highly probable. In scientific evaluations, the number goes up to 10^{15} (quadrillion). When it comes to stating a scientific law, we are told that the number is 10^{50}. In other words, if there is a mathematical probability of something occurring 10^{50} times, with only one chance of failure, the event is said to have been established

---

3   Hugh Ross, *The Creator and the Cosmos* 1993), 115.

by law, meaning it will always occur. Conversely, if there is only one chance of occurrence and 10^{50} chances of failure, the event is considered to be utterly impossible. (Keep these probabilities in mind.) Just to put this in concrete terms, if I were to write the number *1* on a piece of paper every second 10^{20} times, it would take me 1.5 trillion years just to write the number down, just to give you a feeling for how *large* these numbers and probabilities are (100 times the supposed age of the entire universe).

Not only does the fine-tuning need an explanation for its cause but so too does life itself. After all, not only is the universe's existence and fine-tuning attributed to *chance* by the atheist, but so is life. Hubert Yockey, a highly regarded information theorist, has calculated the amount of information content in the minimum genome for life to arise and the probability of that occurring by chance as something less probable than $10^{186,000}$. Harold Morowitz calculated the odds of a whole cell randomly assembling under the most ideal circumstances to be on in $10^{100,000,000,000}$. *Anything greater than 10^{15} is considered beyond possibility remember.* So let us be honest for a moment, who has the most faith? The supporter of the God hypothesis or the supporter of the chance hypothesis?

Here's what an argument from design could look like:

1. The fine-tuning of the universe is due to either necessity, chance, or design.
2. It is not due to necessity or chance.
3. Therefore, it is due to design.

The vast majority of philosophers as well as cosmologists do not believe it is due to necessity simply because there is no reason to believe the universe must have been life-permitting, so you are left with chance or design, and design entails a designer, which is a dirty word in secular academia because it would mean that naturalism is false, so they (again) choose chance as their preferred reason. Again just ask yourself if chance really is a better and simpler explanation than God for not only the beginnings of the universe but also the incredible level of fine-tuning that it took to even make existence or life possible.

Where Does Information Come From?

Have you ever asked yourself where information itself comes from, or what its source is? *Source* means the origin of something. An information source is a source of information for somebody (i.e., anything that might inform a person about something or provide knowledge to somebody). Information sources may be observations, people, speeches, documents, pictures, organizations, etc. They may be primary sources, secondary sources, tertiary sources, and so on.

Different epistemologies have different views regarding the importance of different kinds of information sources. Empiricism regards sense data as the ultimate information sources while other epistemologies have different views. So what is the information source for the blueprint found in all things, including the universe as well as the cell? For example, before a building comes together, there has to be a blueprint of how the building will come together in the first place. It indicates not only how but also where the construction of the building is coming from, but where does the information that leads to the building come from?

1. Information systems come from a mind that designed them.
2. DNA (for example) is the product of a massive information system.
3. Therefore, DNA is from a mind that designed the information system.
4. This mind is best described as God.

You could then go one step further:

5. The best explanation for the identity of this God is the one found in the Bible (see next chapter).

The Moral Argument: Are Morals Objective or Subjective?

When I say *objective*, this means that regardless of what someone says, regardless of geography, culture, tradition, or time, a certain act or action is truly right or wrong. On the other hand, *subjective* is basically one's opinion—that I prefer vanilla ice cream over chocolate, for example. This does not mean vanilla is better tasting than chocolate for everyone in all places and at all times. It is simply my preference. With that being said, are moral values objective or subjective? Is rape, torture, or murder simply subjective? In other words, while we might not like it, there is nothing actually wrong about it; it is simply our preference that is against it (much like the analogy on the flavor of ice cream). Or are such acts truly, objectively wrong? From a Darwinist approach, our minds and society have just accidentally, by chance, evolved in such a way that our societal instincts have deemed such acts as torture, rape, and child abuse wrong, but it isn't really wrong. In other words, if we had evolved a little differently, then such acts might be deemed acceptable.

So the Darwinist/Naturalist once again cannot satisfactorily answer this concern, for they must either say that nothing is wrong with such horrible acts, and that there is no real difference between a Hitler or Mother Teresa, since we just happened to by chance evolve this way. While most will agree this is not a satisfactory conclusion, we must acknowledge if we say that there are truly some things that are right or wrong or good or evil, then we are saying that moral values do have an objective meaning or base ontologically. But if we say this, how is it objective? Just like the information in DNA, this objectiveness of morals had to come from some type of moral lawgiver. For how can morals be objective and not be derived from some type of creator/designer that decided what was right/wrong or good/evil in the first place?

Let me use another example, if the Nazis had won WW2 and executed everyone who said the genocide of the Jews was wrong (so that everyone in the world said that the genocide was good), would this act truly be "good" then? From the Darwinist/Naturalist perspective, the answer would be yes because society, through natural selection, would have changed to say that the killing and torture of a Jewish child is a good act. I believe (and hope) that we all can see that such an act would still be "wrong/evil," even if no one on earth condemned it. It is wrong because the consciousness built into us cries out that such an act is objectively wrong. From the original "source," these are objective and therefore instilled into our blueprint, so to speak, so that love, for example, is an "objectively" good moral.

Dr. Alex Rosenberg (head of ethics at Duke University), who describes himself as a disenchanted naturalist, provides the following summary of atheism's answers to some of life's most persistent questions:

- *Is there a God?* No.
- *What is the nature of reality?* What physics says it is.
- *What is the purpose of the universe?* There is none.
- *What is the meaning of life?* Ditto.
- *Why am I here?* Just dumb luck.
- *Is there a soul?* Are you kidding?
- *Is there free will?* Not a chance!
- *What is the difference between right/wrong, good/bad?* There is no moral difference between them.
- *Does the human past have any lessons for our future?* Fewer and fewer, if it ever had any to begin with.

- *Does history have any meaning or purpose?* It's full of sound and fury, but signifies nothing.
- [He concludes] So much for the meaning of history, and everything else we care about.[4]

So while you are thinking about this, let me make the following observation:

1. If God does not exist, then objective moral values do not exist.
2. Objective moral values do exist.
3. Therefore, God exists.

This is mostly agreed upon by atheists and Christians alike simply because nothing can have objectivity if there is no God as a foundation so, like Alex Rosenberg, he does not "like" the idea of rape or torture of a child, but he cannot say it is wrong because there is no such thing based on his atheistic worldview. So one must assume our existence, the origins of the universe, the origins of life, and the origins of information as well as moral worth are all due to chance if they wish to be atheists, and somehow this is considered an intellectual position whereas "God" is not? I will just leave you with this simple question to ponder: how can anything be right or wrong objectively outside of God?

So what we are left with is the Christian explanation for the world we live in:

- The universe began to exist because God brought it into being as the Bible describes.
- The earth (beyond all probability) landed in the perfect galaxy and formed perfectly (cosmological constants) so

---

4   Alexander Rosenberg, *The Atheist's Guide to Reality* (2011), 3–4.

life could be possible because God designed it for life as the Bible describes.

- Where does information come from (physics of the universe, the applicability of mathematics, DNA/RNA, etc.)? God as creator and the mind behind all of creation as the Bible describes.

- Here is how the Christian explains morals, meaning, and objectivity of the arts: Morals seem real because they are. There is real right and wrong because God is a lawgiver who dictates (ontologically) that some things are right or wrong, good or bad. Similarly God gives us true meaning beyond our own lives here on earth. The arts (from music to painting) are modes we create because we are built in God's image as the Bible describes.

Here is the naturalistic/atheistic explanation:

- The universe began to exist because of chance/accident.

- The earth (beyond all probability) landed in the perfect galaxy and formed perfectly (cosmological constants) so life could be possible because of chance/accident.

- Where does information come from (physics of the universe, the applicability of mathematics, DNA/RNA, etc.)? Chance/accident.

- Here is how atheists explain morals, meaning, and objectivity of the arts: Morals are not real. There is no good or bad because we are just animals that exist by chance, and we have no objective meaning or purpose to our lives or anything we do; it is just all subjective.

Having worked with, visited, and debated with many atheistic groups, graduate students, and professors, I can assure you that they mostly agree with me here (though they will say that they can explain chance better than I have here of course), so I simply ask you (Christian or non-Christian) if chance really is the best option to explain all of this. Similarly the formation of language, writing, and civilization are attributed to chance by the naturalists/atheists, but they are explained as part of God acting within history in the Bible. The more the Christian contemplates these things, the stronger their faith will become, and the more they should ask naturalists: Why cling to chance and purposelessness when you were created for so much more? What do you think about Pascal's Wager? Do you really want to bet against God? What if you're wrong? What if he's right?

Therefore, we should be able to conclude the following:

1. The universe, life, morality, information, and purpose exist in reality through some type of intelligent designer.

2. Genesis and the Bible describe the best and most accurate source of explanation to what this intelligence is.

3. The intelligence described in the Bible as God makes the most logical argument as to why the universe, life, morality, information, and purpose exist in reality.

4. Therefore the intelligent designer is the God of the Bible.

5. Therefore, the Bible can be fully trusted in an explanatory scope and human understanding of ultimate cause, purpose, and destiny (as will be discussed in the next chapter).

You should be able to answer these questions after reading this chapter:

1. Is it possible for life to have objective purpose or meaning without God? Explain.

2. Give a simple example of a deductive argument that has three premises. Are the first two true, and does the third logically follow? Explain.

3. How does the cosmological argument point toward God?

4. What is the teleological argument?
5. How do objective morals make God necessary?

Here are my top 3 recommended readings for a greater understanding this chapter:

1. *The Philosophy of Art: An Introduction to Theism and Aesthetics* by James Stroud (2015)
2. *Philosophical Foundations for a Christian Worldview* by J. P. Moreland and William Lane Craig (2003)
3. *The Privileged Planet: How Our Place in the Cosmos Is Designed for Discovery* by Guillermo Gonzalez and Jay Richards (2004)

> Despite everything, I believe that people are really good at heart.
>
> —Anne Frank

5

Can We Trust the Bible?

> No historian can legitimately rule out documentary evidence simply on the ground that it records remarkable events. If the documents are sufficiently reliable, the remarkable events must be accepted even if they cannot be successfully explained by analogy with other events or by an *a priori* scheme of natural causation.
>
> —John Warwick Montgomery,
> *History, Law, and Christianity*

Picture of the Dead Sea Scrolls that were discovered in the 1940s and provide us with further confirmation that today's Old Testament is accurate when compared to the scrolls that date as far back as 385 BC.

Having done much of my first undergraduate work in history at the University of Arkansas, as well as my master's in ancient history, I have always found it quite alluring that Judaism and Christianity are the only religions that use history to substantiate their claims. Think about it, if God is going to communicate to man, why not do it through mankind's history itself? Islam, for example, believes that the Qur'an describes itself as a book of guidance, rarely offering detailed accounts of specific historical events and often emphasizing the moral significance of an event over its narrative sequence, but it, like most religious texts, is the revelation of *one* witness, that of Mohammad. Buddhist texts are based more on the life and teachings of Siddhartha (Buddha) and his teachings. Hinduism regards the Vedas as a collection of hymns or mantras to be chanted by a priest, the Atharvaveda as a collection of spells and incantations. While all of these books are very interesting they are not based within history.

When we really dive into all other religions and belief systems and their writings, we find the fact that the Bible is the only religious documentation that is steeped in

1. creation/origin science documentation,
2. historic reliability, and
3. prophetic texts.

This means that it can be followed/examined through a historic approach and thus testable (at least through our limited means of evaluation). Therefore, there are ample reasons to spend a few moments in evaluating the historicity and reliability of this text. Christ himself used the Old Testament to point to his fulfillment of these texts, so it is important to quickly evaluate (and be able to explain to others) these three points to see if they hold up to the test. As I have continually repeated, I am not saying anything controversial here. The Bible is the only religious text written in a historic context, which begs the question "why?" By basing it in history, it is real and testable unlike most religions.

One of the first things we must establish is that when we say *biblical manuscripts*, we are using the term for historic writings that were used in piecing together what we now simply call the Bible. Some will argue that because a text was incorporated into the Bible, it now cannot be relied upon to be unbiased, but this is simply false. Scribes copied down these manuscripts in various places, languages, and styles, and then through a painstaking evaluation of these texts, the text of the Bible slowly began to be put together. Therefore, these manuscripts existed independently long before the Bible was put together.

We have already covered premise 1 on the creation story in the first part of the book and concluded that the universe did indeed have a beginning. The creation of the universe, the design we see in nature and life itself, the blueprint in our DNA and morals, the history of mankind, etc., all match up perfectly with Genesis and the Bible as a whole. Many believers and unbelievers alike have commented that the biblical account of creation match precisely with what they observe in their scientific studies.

The biblical account holds up well with step 1, so let's review step 2.

While nowhere in the Bible is there a promise of the purity of text throughout history, there is a great deal of evidence that suggests that the Bibles we read are extremely close to the original. Such reliability helps support the consensus of the Bible being a valuable and accurate account of history as well as revelation from God. We must remember that the Old and New Testaments cover a time span that we can verify with archaeology and other sources from approximately 2,100 BC (Abraham) to the book of Revelation, approximately AD 90, so to keep a faithful written account would indeed prove challenging (and for a more detailed account, I would reference you to my work *The Philosophy of History*). Looking first at the Old Testament, we find that the accuracy of the copies we have is supported by a number of evidence. All of the copies we have agree with the majority of text (some of the copies are more paraphrased than a word-for-word account, so naturally those differ). These also agree with our more modern copies such as the Septuagint (the Greek translation), which dates from the second century BC.

Finally with the discovery of the Dead Sea Scrolls (Hebrew), we are able to compare all of our documents to these scrolls that date as early as 385 BC and provide an almost complete account of the Old Testament.[1] When we compare all of these, we find that all of these translations are extremely close to each other and, furthermore, are extremely close to our modern translations. Most scholars have agreed that these match our current translations by 95 percent, with the 5 percent mostly being variations in spelling that do not alter any themes. This 95 percent accuracy for a document thousands of years old is second to none historically. We also have ancient documents quoting the Old Testament that further increase the reliability of the Old Testament.

Archaeology

Another interesting field of study is that of biblical archaeology. Historians agree that archaeology has consistently and repeatedly confirmed the history of the Old Testament. Many history books have been rewritten after finding archaeological discoveries that proved the biblical story accurate but was not at the time considered accurate by the historian. It is ironic that biblical archaeology really got started about 150 years ago and that its purpose was more for disproving the Bible rather than proving it. But once again, just like scientists and historians, the more archaeologists attempted to disprove the biblical narratives, the more they ended up confirming their truth, thus began a fascinating field of study that not only gives further confirmation of biblical truths but also gives us a real insight as to how these people lived. It is a shame that this study only came about in the last 150 years, or we would even have more historic confirmation at our disposal.

One fascinating book that first reviewed the correlation of Old Testament archaeology with that of history was *The Bible*

---

1   Maxine Grossman, *Rediscovering the Dead Sea Scrolls* (2010), 48–51.

as History by Dr. Werner Keller, whose book sold more than 10 million copies. In it, Dr. Keller traces the Old Testament and New Testament histories through that of confirmed archaeological finds. Little did Dr. Keller know that the next forty years would have a large amount of finds that would further confirm this history. After many of these confirmations, Dr. Keller commented,

> These breathtaking discoveries, whose significance it is impossible to grasp all at once, make it necessary for us to revise our views about the Bible. Many events which previously passed for 'pious tales' must now be judged to be historical. Often the results of investigation correspond in detail with the biblical narratives. They do not only confirm them, but also illumine the historical situations out of which the Old Testament and the Gospels grew.[2]

More recently Dr. J. Randall Price (ThM Old Testament and Semitic languages and PhD in Middle Eastern studies) wrote a book called *The Stones Cry Out* (1997), in which he goes through the basics of biblical archaeology and what it reveals to us about Scripture. While remaining humble on archeology's role, he says,

> According to Webster's English Dictionary, one of the meanings of the word confirm is 'to give new assurance of the validity' of something. Archaeology provides a new assurance of the Bible from the stones to accompany the assurance we already have from the Spirit. The value is an apologetic one, and from the beginning of the science of archaeology, it was a contributing factor in both instigating and sponsoring excavations. Almost all scholars still attest to the significant agreement between the stones and the Scriptures.[3]

---

2 Werner Keller, *The Bible as History: A Confirmation of the Book of Books* (New York: W. Morrow, 1956), 23.

3 Randall Price, *The Stones Cry Out* (Eugene, OR: Harvest House Publishers, 1997), 36.

Once again, I am not going into a lot of details in this booklet. I will just simply say that while questions always remain, we can conclude that archaeology has confirmed the history of the Old Testament, not only in its general outline but in many of the minute details also. For example just over a century ago, scoffers pointed to the Hittite civilization as never existing and the Old Testament just made it up. Then in 1906, Hugo Winckler discovered a royal Hittite archive containing over 10,000 tablets. Needless to say, historians today record the Hittite empire as being much like the Old Testament described it. And aside from the monumental discoveries confirming Old Testament accuracy (example: Siloam inscription, Lachish relief, Moabite stone, Cyrus Cylinder, Tel Dan stele, etc.), we have many historians, such as the late Dr. J. Rufus Fears, who acknowledge the author of the Old Testament's Book of Samuel as being the "Father of History" more than Herodotus. Needless to say the Old Testament is of a superior historic quality and reliability. After the Old Testament period of the Judges, the archeological evidence makes it increasingly clear that the biblical authors knew very well what they were talking about.

New Testament

One area that I have always heard praise for is in the amount of New Testament documents available. I, however, did not realize quite how expansive this collection was in quality as well as quantity. The kinds of witnesses to the New Testament are similar in scope to other historical literature but are incredibly abundant, as even a naturalistic historian such as Bart Ehrman will acknowledge. The most important documents for recovering the most original wording of the New Testament would be the Greek manuscripts since they are the oldest and most common language of the time. To date, we have 5,745 Greek manuscripts divided into four classes according to the materials from which they are made or their particular style of writing.

1. Papyri (118) – Manuscripts written in the AD 2nd to 6th centuries on paper made from the papyrus plant into scrolls and written on with ink.

2. Unicals (317) – Manuscripts written in the AD 4th to 10th centuries in large elegant capital letters that are disconnected from one another, although words were not separated and no punctuation was used. These are written on parchment (goat or sheepskin) or vellum with ink.

3. Minuscules (2877) – Manuscripts written in the AD 9th to 16th centuries in small cursive script, in which the letters are connected to one another.

4. Lectionaries (2433) – Manuscripts composed as early as the first century, in which the books of the New Testament are arranged for daily study and meditation and not according to the canonical order.

The earliest of these are written on papyrus and, though they are fragmentary, date back to about AD 125. This earliest fragment of John 18 is Papyrus 52. It is partially unique because the Gospel of John is universally agreed to be the last of the Gospels written around AD 90–100, so this AD 125 date gets us back very close to the originals. Though there are fifteen of these early papyrus manuscripts, it is not until closer to AD 150 that we get a much more intact set of Greek manuscripts in the Chester Beatty Papyri, which contains fragments of all of the books of the New Testament, including the oldest copy of Luke.

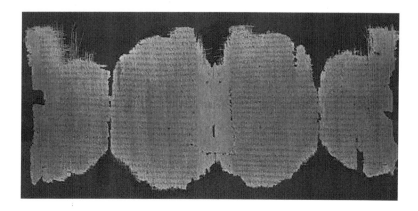

On November 17, 1931, *the London Times* announced the discovery of twelve manuscripts, said to be from a Coptic graveyard in Egypt, stowed away in jars. The documents were subsequently bought by Chester Beatty. This sensational find is of similar importance for New Testament studies as the Dead Sea Scrolls were for Old Testament studies. Among the manuscripts that were found is the earliest surviving collection of the apostle Paul's letters known as P^{46}, which stands for the forty-sixth published NT manuscript on papyri. This collection has been dated by the style of the handwriting as early as the midsecond century (AD 150) and is now housed in the Chester Beatty Library, Dublin.

Only about eighty-five years separate this from the original letters of Paul. This makes the textual witness to the original New Testament unique when compared to other ancient books since it is not unusual for a thousand years or more to separate the lost originals of ancient manuscripts from the first surviving copy. The less the time that has passed, the less opportunity for embellishments to creep into the writings. One of the surviving pages from P^{46} contains a part of Paul's letter to the Corinthian Church (1 Cor. 15:1–6), in which Paul outlines the important message that he announced to them. In this passage, Paul uses technical language to indicate that he was passing on an oral tradition in a fixed form from that even the most ardent of NT critics acknowledges as authentic and dates back to within three to five years of Jesus's crucifixion.

In this creed, Paul summarizes that Christ died for our sins, rose again, and appeared to over five hundred people as well as the apostles. Paul adds that many were still alive at the time of his writing to the Corinthians and could therefore verify the truth of what he wrote. As already mentioned, First Corinthians 15:1–6 has been dated by even the most skeptical of historians to within three to five years of the events themselves and therefore has a firm historical foundation that these four areas were information (that the Gospels espouse upon) already well in circulation right after the crucifixion itself and were therefore not a later invention. For these combined reasons, as well as the rapid spreading of Christianity, most historians believe the complete Bible (at least for the most part) was well in circulation by AD 190.

Alongside these various Greek manuscripts, we have translations from the original Greek into Old Latin, Coptic, Old Syriac, Armenian, Ethiopic, Persian, Gothic, Georgian, Old Slavonic, and Arabic. Obviously the most important of these versions are those that are the earliest (Latin, Coptic, Syriac). These date from the AD 3rd to the 16th centuries, but the texts from which they were translated may go back into the second century. We have approximately 10,000 manuscripts fitting into this Latin category. The Coptic manuscripts number about 1,000 and date from the third to fifth centuries, and the Syriac date to the third century and number well over 1,000.

If we add the other early versions of fourth century Gothic, fifth to sixth century Armenian, Georgian, and Ethiopic, as well as the eighth to ninth century Arabic and Old Slavonic, we have approximately 20,000 total manuscripts for the New Testament. However, one area that as a historian has greatly helped in my studies is that what is often referred to as the church fathers or patristic literature. This material dates as early as the AD 1st century and as late as the thirteenth century, and the number of biblical citations exceeds one million. Many of the church fathers such as Papias, bishop of Hierapolis around AD 130, and Polycarp, bishop of Smyrna, as well as Clement of Rome, were all students of the apostles firsthand according to their writings and the dating of their materials. This does indeed help the historian see the transition from the first into the second century, with Clement writing in AD 96, and through form criticism, we see that there is not any significant changes in meaning or purpose. Papias, Polycarp, and others were students who walked with the apostle John firsthand. We then have Irenaeus, who was a student of Polycarp, and his writings also match what we are told in the Gospels, and so it goes down through history.[4]

Reliability of the New Testament Documents

AUTHOR/BOOK	TIME GAP BETWEEN THE ORIGINAL AND THE COPY	NUMBER OF COPIES
Herodotus, *History*	ca. 1,350 yrs.	109
Thucydides, *History*	ca. 1,300 yrs.	8
Plato	ca. 1,300 yrs.	7
Demosthenes	ca. 1,400 yrs.	200
Caesar, *Gallic Wars*	ca. 1,000 yrs.	31
Livy, *History of Rome*	ca. 400 yrs. ca. 1,000 yrs.	1 partial 19 copies
Tacitus, *Annals*	ca. 1,000 yrs.	251
Pliny Secundus, *Natural History*	ca. 750 yrs.	7
New Testament	fragment of a book: ±50 yrs. books of the NT: 100 yrs. most of the NT: 150 yrs. complete NT: 225 yrs.	5,745 (Greek) 15,000+ (non-Greek) 20,000+ (total)

The point of importance here for the historian is that as we enter into the era of the New Testament, the facts become quite clear and, in all honesty, overwhelming that when it comes to

---

4   Randall Price, *Searching for the Original Bible* (2007).

the New Testament itself, no other ancient writing is even close to being as well attested or documented as the New Testament writings. As mentioned above, we have to date a total of 5,745 Greek manuscripts of the New Testament. When we add the Latin, Ethiopic, Slavic, Armenian, and others, the total exceeds 20,000. Moreover, when we look at the manuscript evidence of other writings such as Caesar's *Gallic Wars*, we have a total of 251 manuscripts to support it. *The History of Herodotus* has 109, and Tacitus's *Annals* has 31. These are not even close to the reliability we have in the New Testament from a textual standpoint, but it does not stop there. Caesar's *Gallic Wars* were written in 100 BC, but the earliest copy we have is dated AD 900, *The History of Herodotus* was written 400 BC, and our earliest copy is dated AD 1000, Tacitus's *Annals* was written in AD 100, and our earliest copy is dated AD 850.[5]

Most historians and critics alike agree that the Gospels were written between AD 45–90 (with Mark being first and John last), and parts of the Pauline Epistles can be dated within ten to fifteen years of Christ's crucifixion. We must also remember these were written by eyewitnesses and attested to multiple times, unlike most other religious texts (for example, no one saw the Buddha have his visions, nor did anyone other than Mohammed witness his revelations from the angel Gabriel). What we have is the most attested ancient documents in history. The fact that we have multiple firsthand accounts from Jesus's followers and that all were written shortly after Jesus's death and resurrection add to its overall credibility. As Ravi Zacharias states,

> In real terms the New Testament is easily the best-attested ancient writing in terms of the sheer number of documents,

---

5 "Updating the Bibliographic Tests for New Testament Documents," last modified September 17, 2012, http://bbhchurchconnection.wordpress.com/2012/09/17/updating-the-bibliographic-test-for-new-testament-documents.

the time span between the events and the document, and the variety of documents available to sustain or contradict it. There is nothing in ancient manuscript evidence to match such textual integrity.[6]

We must remember that I am just scratching the very surface of our evidential criteria. As the brilliant Dr. John Warwick Montgomery also points out, not only do we have the remarkable internal evidence, we also have a plethora of external evidence. For example, while eleven of the twelve apostles were martyred for their faith, John (who walked with Jesus, witnessed his crucifixion firsthand, witnessed his resurrection firsthand, and took care of Mary, the Mother of Jesus until her death) also had (as mentioned earlier) students of his own who wrote down what he said and did.

Historians and literary critiques continue to be amazed by the level of accuracy of the scriptures. Classical scholar and historian Colin Hemer chronicles Luke's accuracy in the book of Acts verse by verse. With painstaking detail, Hemer identifies 84 facts in the last sixteen years of Acts that have been confirmed by historical and archaeological research. Roman historian A. N. Sherwin-White says, "For Acts the confirmation of historicity is overwhelming…Any attempt to reject its basic historicity must now appear absurd. Roman historians have long taken it for granted."[7] We also find another 59 historically confirmed details in the Gospel of John, which, when you add this with John's personal conversations with Jesus, it really does make it seem that it would take more faith to dismiss these than to take them as authentic. When we look merely at the three books of Acts, John, and Luke, we find 140 historically confirmed details, plus the

---

6   Ravi K. Zacharias, *Can Man Live without God?* (Word Publishing, 1994), 162.
7   A. N. Sherwin-White, *Roman Society and Roman Law in the New Testament* (Oxford: Clarendon Press, 1963), 189.

fact that they continually reference historic figures of that time, we can see how this adds further credit to the New Testament's reliability and historicity. Needless to say, to be skeptical of the New Testament is to be skeptical of all history before about AD 1500, for no historic book in both historical quality and quantity rivals the New Testament (secular or religious).

If anyone says, "You're wrong!" Simply ask them what ancient source they consider more credible in either quality or quantity, and you will quickly see how their objections disappear.

Non-Christian Sources on the Historical Jesus

I am often asked if there are any nonbiblical sources for Jesus. First of all it must be pointed out that the plethora of manuscripts we have for Jesus today did not start as a bible but were only later put into what we call the New Testament today. So it must first of all be pointed out that to dismiss any of this manuscript evidence is, in effect, to dismiss the most primary sources we have on the historical Jesus. With that said, we do have corroborating support from strictly non-Christian sources that do help us better confirm the reliability of the New Testament. For the scope of this book, I will only mention the following six non-Christian sources on the historical Jesus:

- Josephus (AD 37–sometime after 100) – Was a Pharisee of the priestly line and a Jewish historian working under Roman authority. He was a Jew and not a follower of Christ, but in his *Antiquities of the Jews*, he had this brief description of a man called Jesus:

    > Now there was about this time Jesus, a wise man, if it be lawful to call him a man, for he was a doer of wonderful works, a teacher of such men as receive the truth with pleasure. He drew over to him both many of the Jews, and many of the Gentiles. And when Pilate, at the suggestion of the principal men among us, had condemned him to the

cross, those that loved him at the first did not forsake him; for he appeared to them alive again the third day; as the divine prophets had foretold these and ten thousand other wonderful things concerning him. And the tribe of Christian so named from him are not extinct at this day.

This from a non-Christian historian. (Josephus also refers to the martyrdom of James, the brother of Jesus, which was not included in the texts of the New Testament, as well as John the Baptist, Herod, and others.)

- Tacitus (AD 56–117) – First-century historian. Tacitus is considered one of the most accurate historians of the ancient world. He wrote,

    Consequently, to get rid of the report, Nero fastened the guilt and inflicted the most exquisite tortures on a class hated for their abominations, called Christians by the populace. Christus, from whom the name had its origin, suffered the extreme penalty during the reign of Tiberius at the hands of one of our procurators, Pontius Pilatus, and a most mischievous superstition, thus checked for the moment, again broke out not only in Judea, the first source of the evil, but even in Rome, where all things hideous and shameful from every part of the world find their center and become popular. (*Annals* 15.44)

The "mischievous superstition" to which Tacitus refers is most likely the resurrection of Jesus. The same is true for one of the references of Suetonius which follows.

- Suetonius – Was chief secretary to Emperor Hadrian (who reigned AD 117–138). He confirms the report recorded in the book of Acts 18:2 that Claudius commanded all Jews to leave Rome in AD 49 (*Life of Claudius*, 25.4). Speaking of the aftermath of the great fire at Rome, Suetonius reports, "Punishment was inflicted on the Christians, a body of people addicted to a novel and mischievous superstition"

(*Life of Nero*, 16). Most historians believe the superstition referred to here is that of the resurrection story.

- Thallus – Wrote around AD 52. He was quoted in reference to the darkness that followed the crucifixion of Christ: "On the whole world there pressed a most fearful darkness, and the rocks were rent by an earthquake, and many places in Judea and other districts were thrown down. This darkness Thallus, in the third book of his History, calls, as appears to me without reason, an eclipse of the sun" (*Chronograph*, 18.1). This is described also in Luke 23:44–45.

- Lucian – Second century Greek writer. He said,

  > The Christians, you know, worship a man to this day—the distinguished personage who introduced their novel rites, and was crucified on that account…You see, these misguided creatures start with the general conviction that they are immortal for all time, which explains the contempt of death and voluntary self-devotion which are so common among them; and then it was impressed on them by their original lawgiver that they are all brothers, from the moment that they are converted, and deny the gods of Greece, and worship the crucified sage, and live after his laws. All this they take quite on faith, with the result that they despise all worldly goods alike, regarding them merely as common property. (*Lucian of Samosata, DP,* 11–13)

- Emperor Trajan – The emperor gave the following guidelines for punishing Christians:

  > No search should be made for these people, when they are denounced and found guilty they must be punished, with the restriction; however, that when the party denies himself to be Christian, and shall give proof that he is not (that is, by adoring our gods), he shall be pardoned on the ground of repentance even though he may have formerly incurred suspicion. (Pliny the Younger, *Letters*, 10:97)

When we only use 100 percent non-Christian/nonbiblical sources of history such as Pliny, Trajan, Lucian, Suetonius, Tacticus, and Josephus, just to name a few, we come up with the following facts about Jesus of Nazareth:

1. Jesus lived during the time of Tiberius Caesar.
2. He lived a virtuous life.
3. He was a wonder worker.
4. He had a brother named James.
5. He was acclaimed to be the Messiah.
6. He was crucified under Pontius Pilate.
7. He was crucified on the eve of the Jewish Passover.
8. Darkness and an earthquake occurred when he died.
9. His disciples believed he rose from the dead.
10. His disciples were willing to die for their belief.
11. Christianity spread rapidly as far as Rome.
12. His disciples denied the Roman gods and worshipped Jesus.[8]

In light of these references, this is yet another affirmation of the New Testament's accuracy on who Jesus was and is.

So while only touching on a few points, we should be able to confidently say that premise 2 on the historical reliability of the Bible, in which we learn about Jesus (and which Jesus used himself—today's Old Testament) has been successfully addressed. No other religion can follow these lines of evidence to the degree of the Bible or Christianity.

---

8 Norman L. Geisler and Frank Turek, *I Don't Have Enough Faith to Be an Atheist* (Wheaton, IL: Crossway Books, 2004).

Our premise 3 is that prophecy is quite unique to the writings of the Bible. Both Old and New Testament have numerous accounts of prophetic messages that are fulfilled. You can say, as the naturalist does in most things, that it is coincidence, chance, or luck, or you can take a more logical approach and begin researching the probabilities of the first two points, see how this begins painting an overwhelming picture of a huge puzzle called purpose or life or existence, and see how they are indeed beginning to form a beautifully complete picture that no other worldview can.

Instead of giving you all of the different prophecies foretelling the coming "Messiah," I will encourage you to research these on your own. His birth, life, and death, all prophesied by many of the different Old Testament prophets, all lead to the fulfillment of the chosen Son of God, the Messiah. This in itself is quite amazing, that through many different individuals throughout the Old Testament, none contradicted one another in their foretelling of the coming Messiah. All are filled by one person in Jesus Christ. (Please remember that we have these prophecies recorded in the Dead Sea Scrolls, which were written well before Jesus of Nazareth was born.) If we take some of these prophecies, it is easy to calculate the probability of someone fulfilling such criteria.

The Mathematical Odds of Jesus Fulfilling All Prophecies

The following probabilities are taken from Peter Stoner in *Science Speaks* to show that coincidence should be ruled out by the science of probability.[9] Stoner says that by using the modern science of probability in reference to eight prophecies, "we find that the chance that any man might have lived down to the

---

9 McDowell, Josh, *The New Evidence That Demands a Verdict* (Nashville, Tennessee: T. Nelson, 1999).

present time and fulfilled all eight prophecies is 1 in 10 to the 17 power." That would be 1 in 100,000,000,000,000,000. In order to help us comprehend this staggering probability, Stoner illustrates it by supposing that "we take 10^{17} silver dollars and lay them on the face of Texas. They will cover all of the state two feet deep. Now mark one of these silver dollars and stir the whole mass thoroughly, all over the state. Blindfold a man and tell him that he can travel as far as he wishes, but he must pick up one silver dollar and say that this is the right one. What chance would he have of getting the right one? Just the same chance that the prophets would have had of writing these eight prophecies and having them all come true in any one man."[10]

Stoner considers 48 prophecies and says, "We find the chance that any one man fulfilled all 48 prophecies to be 1 in 10^{157}, or 1 in 100,000,000,000,000,000,000,000,000,000,000,000,000, 000,000,000,000,000,000,000,000,000,000,000,000,000,00 0,000,000,000,000,000,000,000,000,000, 000, 000,000,000,000 ,000,000,000,000,000,000,000,000,000. The estimated number of electrons in the universe is around 10 to 79th. It should be quite evident that Jesus did not fulfill the prophecies by accident."

Remember from earlier that anything greater than 10^{15} is beyond possibility. (Just as a test, I *highly* encourage you to read Isaiah 53 or to Google "Jesus fulfilled prophecies" so you will gain a sense of these Old Testament prophecies speaking about Jesus Christ.)

So while the naturalist or naturalistic historian will still scream, "Another lucky chance/coincidence," I think Christianity has successfully fulfilled all three of these premises, so we can conclude the following:

1. Any document that can be confirmed to be accurate through creation, historicity, and prophecy would be the

---

10 Ibid.

most reliable document in existence and could be fully trusted.
2. The Bible fulfills this criteria
3. Therefore, the Bible can be fully trusted.

One may argue with these points, but they must once again disprove the three points as I have lined them out or present a more probable hypothesis (please encourage non-Christians to formulate a better hypothesis for each than luck or chance). So you might ask, Why then do so many now argue against Christianity? Some are simply due to Christians giving Christ such a bad name, they are disgusted with the entire "religious" thing, and most have presuppositions or biases against the miracles discussed in the New Testament or on the resurrection of Christ. When discussing a non-naturalistic miracle or the Resurrection, we must remember that scientists are out of their fields on this subject, and we must turn to the historian or philosopher. For example, science can show that it is possible that the Nazis could have come through the Ardennes forest to launch a stealth attack against the Allied forces, but it cannot prove they did. Therefore, we must look to history. Historic evidences included could be witnesses, written documentation, dates of written composition, supporting texts from different sources, and archaeology, to name just a few.

A great example of the limits of science and naturalism can be seen when philosopher and theologian William Lane Craig debated the staunch Darwinist Peter Atkins.

> ATKINS. Everything in the world can be understood without needing to evoke a God. You have to accept that's one possible view to take about the world.
>
> CRAIG. Sure, that's possible, but—
>
> ATKINS. Do you deny that science can account for everything?
>
> CRAIG. Yes, I do deny that science can account for everything.
>
> ATKINS. So what can't it account for?

Craig calmly said he would just name five:

1. Mathematics and logic – Science cannot prove them because science presupposes them.

2. Metaphysical truths – such as, there are minds that exist other than my own (Ex: *The Matrix*).

3. Ethical judgments – You cannot prove by science that the Nazis were evil because morality is not subject to the scientific method.

4. Aesthetic judgments – The beautiful, like the good, cannot be scientifically proven.

5. Science itself – The belief that the scientific method discovers truth cannot be proven by the scientific method itself.

(Atkins had no immediate response other than a somewhat dumbfounded look on his face.)

With this being said, we must dismiss our presuppositions and prejudices against such things as "miracles" and just see what the best hypothesis surrounding Christ's resurrection is.

We will only touch on a few to see how credible the resurrection is and why you should be able to easily share this with a skeptic (as well as quell any of your own doubts).

The Resurrection of Christ Makes Sense

How do we know from a historical perspective that Jesus rose from the dead? When working on my undergraduate studies in history at the University of Arkansas, I began to see how historians put together their information from past events to arrive at a working cumulative case argument from the facts at hand. When we take this same approach with an agnostic or skeptic, we have no real choice (regardless of our preferences) but to take the facts as they are and see where the supporting facts lead us. So in light of the question concerning a skeptic asking how we know that Jesus rose from the dead, we should approach it the same way we would if someone asked us, "How do you know Alexander the Great never lost a battle?" And that is by taking the most agreed-upon established historic facts and then going down the list of the less established facts until we can arrive at a consensus or the best explanation for our conclusions so that our conclusions form the best hypothesis (over competing ones) for the specific claim being evaluated. Here are just three of the established facts (which for the most part, are agreed upon by critic and non-critic alike) concerning the facts around Jesus's death:

1. The empty tomb
2. The postmortem appearances
3. The origin of the Christian faith

We will briefly review these three claims:

The empty tomb. The tomb must have been empty because the disciples could not have believed in Jesus's resurrection if his corpse still lay in the tomb. Also, Jews or Romans could have simply presented the body before the populace to quell any dispute about the missing corpse. One of the most remarkable facts about the early Christian belief in Jesus's resurrection was that it flourished in the very city where Jesus had been publicly crucified. Few would have been prepared to believe such nonsense that Jesus had been raised from the dead if they had not had a real reason to justify this belief. I will paraphrase Dr. William Lane Craig in pointing to the fact that Jesus's burial is attested in extremely early independent sources multiple times.[11]

The account of Jesus's burial by Joseph of Arimathea is part of Mark's (Gospel) source material, this being a very early source,

---

11 See www.ReasonableFaith.org debates, discussions, articles by William Lane Craig, which much of is paraphrased here.

which is probably based on eyewitness testimony and which some critics date to within seven years of Jesus's crucifixion. Moreover, Paul in 1 Corinthians 15:3–5 quotes a much older Christian tradition that he had received from the earliest disciples (within the first five years of Jesus's death): "that Christ died for our sins in accordance with the Scriptures, and that He was buried, and that He was raised on the third day in accordance with the Scriptures, and that He appeared to Cephas, then to the Twelve." For these reasons, most New Testament critics agree that Jesus was buried by Joseph of Arimathea in a tomb, and it is one of the earliest and best-attested facts about Jesus. If this conclusion is correct, then it seems very difficult to deny the historicity of the empty tomb.

The postmortem appearances. Once again, looking at the very early letters of 1 Corinthians 15:3–8 (ESV):

> For I delivered to you as of first importance what I also received, that Christ died for our sins in accordance with the scriptures, and that he was buried, and that he was raised on the third day in accordance with the scriptures, and that he appeared to Cephas, then to the Twelve. Then he appeared to more than five hundred brethren at one time, most of whom are still alive, though some have fallen asleep. Then he appeared to James, then to all the apostles. Last of all, as to one untimely born, he appeared also to me.

If we briefly break this down, it tells us that Jesus appeared to Peter, to all of the apostles, to more than five hundred brethren, to James, and finally to Paul. If we go straight to the five hundred, we find something quite amazing. Paul reports that "most are still alive," which is basically saying, "They are witnesses too, so don't hesitate to go ask them as well" (this would also help explain why a huge populace of the city believed in the resurrection instead of just a handful of fanatics). Also what is very interesting is James, Jesus's brother, seemed to not believe in Jesus's messiahship. After Jesus's alleged resurrection, however, James became a large player and instrument in the early church and, as recorded by the Jewish historian Josephus, was martyred for his faith in Christ, which he would not deny even though it could have saved his life if he had (Josephus, *Antiquities of the Jews*). Then finally, He appeared to a well-trained Jewish Pharisee, Saul of Tarsus, who was a vehement persecutor of the early Christian church. This is only a very brief sketch, but we are once again building a cumulative case argument that is increasingly convincing and hard to dispute.

The origin of the Christian Faith. Even the most critical of New Testament scholars hold that the disciples at least did witness what they "thought" was the resurrected Jesus. It is becoming increasingly difficult to admit that the early and rapid growth of the Christian faith could be attributed to anything else. Jewish tradition had always held to a Messiah that would come in triumphantly to establish the throne of David, not one who would shamefully be executed by them as a criminal. It is difficult to imagine what a disaster the crucifixion was for the disciples' faith. Jesus's death on the cross must have looked like a humiliating end for any hopes entertained that he was the Messiah, but the belief in the resurrection of Jesus reversed the catastrophe of the crucifixion because God had raised Jesus from the dead as he had foretold, he was seen to be the Messiah after all. This is why the majority of all attempts to explain away the resurrection have collapsed.

The origin of Christianity owes itself to this belief held by the earliest disciples that God had raised Jesus from the dead. This belief cannot be plausibly accounted for in terms of either Christian, pagan, or Jewish influences. As Dr. Craig points out,

> Even if we grant, for the sake of argument, that the tomb was somehow emptied and the disciples saw hallucinations—suppositions which we have seen to be false anyway—the origin of the belief in Jesus' resurrection still cannot be plausibly explained. Such events would have led the disciples to say only that Jesus had been translated into heaven, not

resurrected. The origin of the Christian faith is therefore inexplicable unless Jesus really rose from the dead.[12]

It is the historian's goal, using all his or her critical skills, to determine what happened in the past by reconstructing it on the basis of evidence. As Fredrick Copleston states in *On the History of Philosophy*, "The historian is not free to interpret the texts as he likes. Some statements may be ambiguous; but there are others, the meaning of which is clearly determined independently of the historian's will."[13]

It is not up to the historian to rule out the resurrection simply because they feel personally that miracles such as the resurrection do not fit their presuppositional beliefs. Therefore, based on the above-mentioned relatively noncontroversial facts, plus the confirmed facts by both firsthand and later witnesses to the events, we can confidently say that if one has any confidence in history whatsoever, then they have little to no reason to doubt (or be agnostic to) the historicity of the resurrection of Christ as the best explanation and hypothesis to the events surrounding Christ's death, the empty tomb, the postmortem appearances, and the very origin of the Christian faith. Considered by many to be the best New Testament historian alive today, Nicholas Wright concludes that the empty tomb and postmortem appearances of Jesus have a historical probability so high as to be "virtually certain," like the death of Augustus Caesar in AD 14 or the fall of Jerusalem in AD 70.[14]

One might still say, "Well, I don't think miracles are a very good explanation," but we must remind them that that type of statement is a philosophical statement (which I had to

---

12 William Lane Craig, *Reasonable Faith*, 395.
13 Frederick C. Copleston, *On the History of Philosophy and Other Essays* (London: Search Press, 1979).
14 N. T. Wright, *The Resurrection of the Son of God* (Minneapolis: Fortress, 2003), 710.

continually remind my history department during my master's studies), and that is irrelevant to what we know concerning the historic facts around Christ's crucifixion. As resurrection critic and non-Christian Wolfhart Pannenberg admitted to William Lane Craig:

> The facts that an event bursts all analogies to the present cannot be used to dispute its historicity. When, for example, myths, legends, illusions, and the like are dismissed as unhistorical, it is not because they are unusual but because they are analogous to present forms of consciousness to which no historical reality corresponds. When an event is said to have occurred for which no present analogy exists, we cannot automatically dismiss its historicity.[15]

Much like Pannenberg admitted, we must look at the facts with an unbiased approach, and when we do, skeptic and agnostic alike must come to the acknowledgement that all arrows do squarely point and attest to the resurrection of Christ as the best hypothesis. Whether it is true or not is irrelevant to the strict historian because he or she is simply reporting the facts as they stand, much like it is not the historian's responsibility to rule out Alexander the Great never losing a battle because of its very unlikelihood (none of the great military leaders throughout history have ever died undefeated in battle and made such an impact as Alexander). Nonetheless, if we interpret the facts with an unbiased approach, we must accept the fact that Alexander the Great was undefeated in battle, and that the resurrection of Jesus by far stands out as the best hypothesis surrounding the three facts mentioned above.

---

15. William Lane Craig, *Reasonable Faith: Christian Truth and Apologetics* (Wheaton, Illinois: Crossway Books, 1994), 153.

You should be able to answer these questions after reading this chapter:

1. How does archaeology help support the Bible? What are some examples?
2. What the odds of Jesus fulfilling all of the Old Testament prophecies about himself by chance? Why is this important?
3. How many total manuscripts do we have in the New Testament, and how accurate are they when compared to our New Testament today? Why does this matter, and what does it tell us?
4. On top of the manuscripts, do we have extra biblical support for the New Testament?
5. Is the resurrection of Jesus a viable historic event? Why or why not?
6. Why is the Bible considered so accurate historically?

Here are my top 3 recommended readings for a greater understanding this chapter:

1. *The Case for Christ: A Journalist's Personal Investigation of the Evidence for Jesus* by Lee Strobel (1998)
2. *The Historical Jesus: Ancient Evidence for the Life of Christ* by Gary R. Habermas (1996)
3. *I Don't Have Enough Faith to Be an Atheist* by Norman L. Geisler, Frank Turek, and David Limbaugh (2004)

6

What about Religions Other Than Naturalism?

> Everyone—pantheist, atheist, skeptic, polytheist—has to answer these questions: 'Where did I come from? What is life's meaning? How do I define right from wrong and what happens to me when I die?" Those are the fulcrum points of our existence.
>
> —Ravi Zacharias

While once again the topic of comparative religion is *far* beyond the scope of any book like this, which has been challenged to cover the basic tenants of Christianity in less than 200 pages. What I will attempt in this chapter is give you a short and concise answer that virtually all critics and noncritics alike agree to in regard to these religious worldviews and will give you an idea of their limited scope in light of Christian theism.

Basic Outline of Facts versus Religions
Ultimate Reality/God

If we trace the Bible back to its origins, we find that people such as Adam, Eve, Noah, etc., were much earlier than any known religion today such as Judaism or Hinduism. The importance lies in the fact that since all of these religions trace themselves back to a great flood that matches the Noah's ark description, we see that after the scattering of nations during the Table of Nations episode, all groups split up and went their own way. With this, obviously some changes to religion would happen over time. The question is: "Which religion most accurately describes *God* at the time of Noah and would thus be closer to the original *source* material that all religions are derived?

1. **Judaism** – By most definitions, is the oldest religion with the call of Abraham (approximately 2100 BC). Leaders such as Abraham, Isaac, Jacob, Moses, David, etc., had to find or discover their calling (they did not know it before God revealed it to them). They all sinned as all humans do, and all pointed toward an eventual Messiah. (There are approximately 12 million practicing Jews today.)

2. **Hinduism** – Some consider this the oldest religion since its writings are closer to 1500 BC, with Moses writing the Torah slightly after this, but as far as pure religion (with the call of the leader Abraham), Judaism is the oldest by several centuries. At its core, Hinduism was monotheistic and believed in only one God, which they called the ultimate reality, known as "truth" (Brahman). After the feeling of not being able to relate to this "ultimate reality," a type of subdeities was created to pray with in order for them to relate to this "God" that was beyond their comprehension (similar to Roman Catholicism's saints and icons). It has no official founder but is a type of evolving religion with a multitude of variances that

can be interpreted as pantheistic and polytheistic as it has drifted away from its original "one God" origins. (There are approximately 1 billion Hindus today.)

These are the two core religions that can trace themselves back the furthest, with Judaism being steeped in human history, so it can be verified, whereas Hinduism cannot. Much of Hinduism is in Sanskrit and cannot be read or interpreted today. Moreover, Hinduism will often describe gods fighting each other, which cannot be verified since it is "outside" of history while Judaism (the Old Testament) is "inside" or within history and can therefore be tested and reviewed.

3. **Buddhism** – It originated from Hinduism when a prince named Siddhartha Gautama left his worldly possessions to find "truth" and concluded that Hinduism did not have the truth because it had drifted so far from its original source. It had created caste systems where priests were higher than commoners and could thus exploit them (similar to early Roman Catholicism). Buddha has been referred to as the Martin Luther of Hinduism, who broke away from the caste system separating the poor from the rich to say that all are able to find enlightenment. Buddhism is traced back to this one individual who himself said he had no authority but could offer advice on how to live lives of meaning without a religious institution per se. Buddha (which means awakened one) repeatedly told his followers that he was just a man and not to treat him as a god, but many did this shortly after his death and continue to today. (There are various branches of Buddhism, with some being more atheistic/agnostic as was Siddhartha. Theravada and Mahayana are the main branches, but there are also many others, such as Zen, Tibetan, Tiantai, Nichiren, etc.) (There are approximately 400 million Buddhists today.)

4. **Christianity** – This considers itself the completion of Judaism because of the fact that Jesus of Nazareth is the promised Messiah, not a prophet, sage, or wiseman alone, such as other religious leaders, but God incarnate (for lack of better terminology) as traced through Judaism. In Judaism, we see God's essence in the burning bush on Mount Sinai, in between the cherubim on the Ark of the Covenant, which was in the Jewish Tabernacle, and then King Solomon's Temple, and finally, as the prophets foretold, born from the womb of a virgin (Mary) into a human temple of flesh. Judaism saw God incarnate within the Torah, the Ark, and through such venues as the pillar of smoke that led the Hebrews from Egypt. Likewise, Christianity saw this same incarnation in Jesus of Nazareth. Jesus said he had come to fulfill the laws of Judaism and the words of the prophets who all wrote of him. The fact that Jesus fulfilled all of the prophecies of the Hebrew Judaic (Old) Testament and died and was resurrected—giving credence as the only religion that we are saved by God's grace, not by our works to God—make Jesus's claims higher than that of any other religion. (There are approximately 1.75 billion Christians today but most are not practicing.)

5. **Islam** – The youngest of the major religions (approximately AD 600) in which one person, Mohammad, saw revelations from an angel, and over one hundred years after his death, some of his followers put together a book of his revelations that is known today as the Koran (or Q'uran). The Koran gives credence that Jesus of Nazareth was the Messiah and will come again at the end of time, but the Koran is not historic and cannot be tested. Similar to Islam, religions such as Montanism (second century) and Manichaeism (third century). Both stated they had "prophets" and a "new revelation" and for a time gathered many adherents,

but when people started debating various truths, these religions soon disappeared when it was realized their beliefs were in contradiction to the beliefs of Christianity. Islam similarly stated they had a new "prophet" six hundred years later and took many of the Bible's characters, but unlike other religions, Islam had combined religion and state and thus Islam had an army to enforce its claims. Islam spread much of its influence by war and conquest and within one hundred years of Mohammed's death, the armies of Islam had conquered the Christian Byzantine territories of modern-day Israel, all of Northern Africa, and crossed into Spain. According to the Koran, non-Muslims have the choice of taxation (a tax for being non-Muslim) as well as second-class status, expulsion, or death. This is built into their very governmental form of Sharia (Islamic) Law and the reason why today no churches, synagogues, Buddhist temples, etc., are allowed in Muslim lands such as Saudi Arabia and today if a Muslim attempts to leave Islam, they can be killed (Pakistan, Afghanistan, Saudi Arabia, Iran, and many other countries have laws built into their constitution mandating death for those who leave Islam. I have not only studied this in great detail but have had the opportunity to work with many persons from these countries).[1]

Muslim moderate and respected leader Yusuf al-Qaradawi admitted in February 2013: "If they [Muslims] had gotten rid of the punishment [often death] for apostasy, Islam would not exist today."[2] This statement begs the question, why (if the Koran is true) do they need to enforce a death penalty in order to keep Muslims from leaving Islam? The Koran does include many stories

---

1 See www.TheLollards.org for more information on Islam's history.
2 http://www.gatestoneinstitute.org/3572/islam-apostasy-death.

from both the Old and New Testaments, but it limits their importance, and the Koran is not chronological but simply makes statements randomly concerning Noah, for example. The Koran's basis is that of Mohammad being the final and greatest prophet. For this reason, Islam (like Mormonism) is a direct offshoot of Christianity; however, there is much in the Koran that contradicts both the Old and New Testaments. The Koran attests that Mohammad (just like all prophets) lived a sinful life but testifies that Jesus lived a pure life. It is very unique to see one religion testifying on the behalf of another religion in Jesus Christ, and this gives an immediate dialogue for conversation. (There are approximately 1.5 billion Muslims today. Many Muslim countries outlaw the practice of any other religion in their country and force their citizens to practice Islam upon threat of death. See www.Persecution.com, in which I am an area representative.)[3]

So based on this simple summary of the five major religions, we should be able to see how they interrelate to one another and how they do have similarities when we consider their origin from Noah's sons following the great flood and then the original religion changing over time away from its original form. We still have new religions that promise "new" light, such as Mormonism or Iglesia ni Cristo, and there will continue to be, but covering these in great detail is far beyond the scope or purpose of this simple book.

My hope is that we can simply see that the claims of Jesus are unmatched and that they continue the story of Judaism (Old

---

3   I mean this with the utmost respect, but Islam is probably the weakest historically as well as philosophically of the great religions. How anyone can say that historically Islam has great plausibility is mind-boggling. See for example *Did Muhammad Exist?* by Robert Spencer or *The Cross in the Shadow of the Crescent* by Erwin Lutzer for more information on Islam's origins.

Testament) and climax with Judaism's promised Messiah of both Jew and Gentile. These do make sense in light of a global flood in which many people were dispersed. The stories they knew about the one true God and why God chose the Jewish nation to preserve the true story until the Messiah came would have changed over the centuries. Therefore, both the Old and New Testaments together give one a complete picture of God through Christ and provide a huge window on how we can relate to a Hindu, Buddhist, and Muslim. For example, many Christians can learn much about prayer and meditation from a Buddhist, and Buddhists can then learn about the enlightened one named Jesus, who did speak with authority while the Buddha said he had no authority. If we show love and respect, we can teach and learn much from other religions and cultures as we share (not force) the Good News of who Jesus of Nazareth was and is and who he represents.

What Is So Unique about Christianity and Christ?

Dr. Subodh Pandit (www.SearchSeminars.org).

At this point, I would like to follow along my good friend Dr. Subodh Pandit's[4] same journey of inquiry, which he describes in

---

4   Dr. Subodh Pandit, *Cross Examination: The Evidence for Belief*, 2011.

his search seminar series and book, and quickly tie this in with other religious thoughts and how they match up in contrast. Dr. Pandit and I have worked together on three events (2008, 2009, and 2014). In his seminars (and book), he describes his ten-year journey searching for God, and then after coming to the conclusion that there must be a God, he describes how he spent another ten years searching through the major religions to conclude that biblical Christianity is the only true way. I will simply follow a similar pattern as Dr. Pandit in laying out the facts and remind each of us that any religion not willing to examine itself will gain a following only through intimidation and fear:

- Hinduism – They have no single founder, and the highest claim is to be that of a sage.
- Islam – Mohammed was called the Seal of the Prophets.
- Buddhism – They have the super enlightened one, who was enlightened in stages while under a fichus tree in India.
- Christianity – Jesus didn't claim to just show truth but to actually be truth as the Son of God thus speaking in the name of God himself.

Obviously, all of these are very prestigious roles, but only one is an out-of-this-world claim.

All are recognized as being in the grave except Jesus.

- Only Buddha witnessed his enlightenment.
- The authors of the Hindu scriptures wrote what was handed down to them. They did not experience the actual stories themselves.
- Only Mohammad saw the angel Gabriel and interpreted these visions. Islam's claims are solely based on Mohammad's witness by later authors.

- Christianity hosts at least forty authors through vast periods of times, from kings to peasants, all parallel in their complete message being fulfilled by the one prophesied of in Jesus Christ. The apostles and disciples of Christ did not only hear about Christ, they actually walked with and lived with Him firsthand.

All major religious figures had to find their journey and purpose.

- Buddha had to search for enlightenment and test out various practices within Hinduism first.
- Mohammed was shown the Word. He did not have it. It had to be revealed to him.
- Jesus knew from His birth what His purpose and mission was.

All religious texts state that their founders sinned except for Jesus, who they claimed was without sin.

The beginnings of the great leaders, their ministry, and death differed.

- Hinduism – While there is no single founder, all appear to have been revered individuals, with honor and prestige surrounding them.
- Buddhism – Gautama Buddha was a prince.
- Islam – Mohammed was of the tribe of Quraysh, which was very important because it was the guardian of the Kaba, the most sacred site in the peninsula.
- Christianity – Jesus was born in a stable among farm animals.

Christ was the only one born in poverty-stricken circumstances. He is also the only one born a virgin birth, which both the New Testament and the Koran testify to.

The leaders' deaths were quite different as well.

- Hinduism – Their deaths were regarded as significant losses to be lamented over for generations as their lives were recounted over and over again (highly celebrated).

- Buddhism – Buddha's body was wrapped in one thousand layers of finest Benares cloth and cremated. He was honored and his followers left to continue his work of searching for enlightenment (highly celebrated).

- Islam – Umar, one of the prominent leaders, hurried ashen-faced to the mosque to mourn and express their great respect and admiration. Mohammed had built the framework for the juggernaut of the caliphate that would later sweep the world and bring almost every opposition to its knees (highly celebrated).

- Christianity – Jesus was tried as a criminal, tortured, beaten, and convicted. He died with two robbers. His disciples having abandoned him. He died as a criminal. (Movement was crushed and ended until the resurrection three days later. Christianity would remain illegal and heavily persecuted for three hundred years. Today (2015) it is still illegal in fifty-three countries in the world.)

When we look at the various religions from a number of perspectives, it is quite amazing how different they are. While I would never purposely mean to disrespect anyone's tradition or religious leaders, we can see that Christ stands out as not of this world in His life of nonmaterialism, His non-earthly empire, His nonprestigious death, and more so in His resurrection.

It is quite amazing when you piece together what philosophers call a cumulative case argument, where you put all the facts together to form the best hypothesis, how Christ stands out so predominantly. Even my Muslim friends do not deny this. It is amazing that from these poor surroundings in an area of the world not deemed particularly important, this Jewish rabbi makes sense of all things in and out of the world.

- Christ's resurrection story grew rapidly in the very town where he was crucified.
- James (Jesus's brother) did not believe in him fully until his resurrection (which tells us something drastic happened to make your own doubting family believe you truly were the Messiah), then he became so devout in his belief that he died rather than deny him (see Josephus).
- All the apostles except for John were martyred for their faith. All they could get from following the Lord was torture, persecution, and eventual martyrdom, but they followed and never doubted him again after the resurrection.
- Hinduism considers Jesus a god/avatar. Many within Buddhism hold him to be a true model to follow, stating that he did reach the ultimate stage of Nirvana. Islam holds him to be the Messiah, saying that he lived a pure and righteous life, was born of a virgin, and that he will come back at the end of the age. Christianity holds him as the invisible expression of God himself who died for our sins and will come back at the end of age. Atheism and agnosticism often hold him as a model moral teacher. (These facts alone are truly remarkable and leave all types of inroads to share with other religions.)

It is indeed amazing that one person in the history of the world stands out like this individual. We even divide history and time (BC/AD) based on him.

Nothing I have discussed in this chapter is overly controversial, and even the majority of skeptics will agree with my points. (I did my master's in history based on this same material at a secular university, and even though many of the professors did not like where my conclusions pointed, they did agree that the facts speak for themselves.)

Moreover, nothing I have discussed in this chapter is that difficult or complicated to learn; therefore, there is no reason why all Christians do not at least know these basic facts about God, Christ, and the faith they profess. In accordance with 1 Peter 3:15 (NASB): "Always being ready to make a defense to everyone who asks you to give an account for the hope that is in you, yet with gentleness and reverence." This is going to be increasingly important in an increasingly secular and post-Christian world and if we want to have any chance of providing all facts to our young adults and future leaders. So as my good friend Dr. Pandit concludes in his book, "May the God of Truth guide you and bring you safely to the harbor of fulfillment and meaning in your life."

The most important thing that we must not let ourselves lose track of is that of having a real relationship with Christ. This is the true theism of Christianity. The most important part of this journey is to know and accept the person of Christ and follow him. While there is nothing I can say to convince you of this, I can testify that the experiential relationship I have with Christ is real, and I encourage you to explore the realness of this for yourselves, for Christ promises if you will just ask him to make himself known to you, he will. I pray that you will have this personal acceptance and relationship with him and understand what that means for you personally through the guidance of the Holy Spirit, which will lead to baptism, finding a good biblical church for worship and fellowship, Bible studies, etc.

So basically, what we are looking at is while secular philosophies and interpretations of science change regularly, to say the least, Christ and the Bible have not. What is more surprising in some ways is the fact that the Bible, while remaining unchanged, has given us an accurate interpretation of the world around us. From the beginnings of space and time in what is now recognized as the big bang, the rapid creation of life (often referenced in the Cambrian explosion), the rapid sophistication in which humans came into existence in the approximate regions of Sumeria/Mesopotamia, history as we know it, all climaxed with time literally being divided with Jesus Christ coming into the scene (BC/AD). All match the biblical narratives and the natural and moral theology all around us. So what do we expect to see in the future? If history repeats, naturalistic theories will come and go, with atheists continuing to claim, "We have it figured out now!" while the Bible and Jesus's words remain the same, timeless, and once again, we will reflect on the truth of the assessment Robert Jastrow ends his book *God and the Astronomers*:

> It is not a matter of another year, another decade of work, another measurement, or another theory; at this moment it seems as though science will never be able to raise the curtain on the mystery of creation. For the scientist who has lived by his faith in the power of reason, the story ends like a bad dream. He has scaled the mountains of ignorance; he is about to conquer the highest peak; as he pulls himself over the final rock, he is greeted by a band of theologians who have been sitting there for centuries.[5]

Afterthoughts: Can We Learn from Other Faiths?

One thing to note is that the church and Christ do not always match (though church as the body of believers is very important). In other words, Christ is truth, but unfortunately the church and all its thousands of denominations do not always have the truth (hence the term *church-ianity*). But do not be turned off from church fellowship (and do not judge Christ by the Christians, but judge the Christians by Christ). I have found other religions are more sound on some features of "experiencing God" when

---

5   Robert Jastrow, *God and the Astronomers* (1978) 115–16.

looking at Christ and how we approach him and therefore can open up much dialogue between us all. Here is an example:

1. **Hinduism** – It states that finite beings (you and I) cannot properly understand the one and true infinite being known as God (Brahman) in mere words/research. This is technically true, but whereas Hindus have developed subdeities much like Roman Catholics have saints, Christ has revealed the infinite God to us in a way that we can at least in a small way begin to understand the infinite. Hindus use statues in the form of subdeities (such as Krishna, Shiva, etc). This leaves an open door to share with them how we approach the infinite God through Jesus Christ. We must remember that although true Christian theology is sound—I can confirm what they are saying in the fact that our theology is the best "attempt" to explain God on paper and in words, and as the prophets of old, such as Amos/Isaiah, can attest to, they did the best they could in communicating God's message to them in words and actions—this does not mean that our "words" can properly encompass the infiniteness of God. The prophets alluded to this point as well. Either way, the door is open to communicate to a Hindu about the one and true God through the person of Jesus of Christ, a.k.a. God Incarnate, which they are often eager to hear about.

2. **Buddhism** – A type of reformed Hinduism in which Siddhartha Gautama abandoned the tradition/hierarchy/rituals of Hinduism (that are also commonplace in our own nonbiblical churches today) because they are man-made attempts to reach the infinite. Siddhartha reached the conclusion that one must free themselves of worldly pursuits and focus on doing good to all things, loving all things, observing equality, and searching inside our very being for the kingdom of God. Siddhartha (the Buddha)

admitted, however, that he was no authority, that only the infinite is the authority. On all of the above accounts, Buddha was correct, and he was in agreement with Christ's teaching on our bodies being full of the Holy Spirit, yet Christ spoke as one "with" authority from God himself. This too can serve as a great bridge for open dialogue and sharing the story of Jesus the Christ with a Buddhist (Jesus is the answer—not a specific church creed or dogma as I have learned from various persecuted Christians from the churches of the east).

More could be said, but one thing that the Eastern religions like Hinduism/Buddhism have helped me to remember is that although all evidences do seem to be stacked heavily on the side of Christian theism (namely in the person of Jesus Christ), we must not be so engrossed with scholarship, logic, and reason that we miss the much bigger picture of meditating on and experiencing God personally. This is a much greater concept of exploration than using calculations, logic, and scholastic endeavors, which are in and of themselves finite and will never be able to fully grasp the infinite as our Hindu/Buddhist brothers and sisters point out.

This experience of Christ/Holy Spirit is what Christ (and Paul later) was referring to when in Luke 17:21 (KJV), Jesus states, "The kingdom of God is within you." Not only must we not lose sight of this inner working that is not explainable, but we can also use this as a stepping stone to discuss Christ within a context that not only Christ used but that a Buddhist or Hindu would also understand perfectly in a loving, friendly, nonforceful (Christ-like) manner. (Please note, I am in no way endorsing other religions, nor am I endorsing any type of liberal way of thinking. I come from a very conservative church mentality, and though I disdain/do not believe in "denominations," I myself do find that a biblical church is usually a conservative one, though conservative is also often times hypocritical. I work with many different groups of Christians, however, and I simply refer to myself as Christian, nothing more and nothing less. My point is that we must simply not miss the forest for the trees in pointing toward Christ as many may be closer than we are whether we (or they) realize it or not.)

Conclusions

In summary, I will use William Lane Craig's (whom I had the privilege of traveling with to Italy, Greece, and Turkey in 2013 on retracing Paul's travels) five premises[6] and add a sixth.[7] We should all be willing to acknowledge these as good reasons to think that the God of Christianity exists:

1. God makes sense of the origin of the universe
2. God makes sense of the fine-tuning of the universe for intelligent life.
3. God makes sense of where and how all information originated
4. God makes sense of objective moral values in the world.
5. God makes sense of the life, death, and resurrection of Jesus Christ.
6. God can be immediately known and experienced.

These are only a very small part of the evidences for God's existence, of course. Alvin Plantinga, one of America's leading philosophers, has laid out two dozen or so arguments for God's existence. Together, these constitute a powerful cumulative case for the existence of God and for the fact that Jesus the Christ is the most accurate understanding of this ultimate reality that finite humans can understand and experience.

---

6 See www.ReasonableFaith.org.
7 A seventh one could be: "God makes sense of aesthetics and the arts" as I cover in my short work *The Philosophy of Art* as well.

You should be able to answer these questions after reading this chapter:

1. I believe in God, but why should I believe in Christ?
2. What are some characteristics of the other major religions (Islam, Hinduism, Buddhism)?
3. What is different about Jesus's life and his claims compared to theirs?
4. Is the Bible the only religious writing that is historic in its nature and therefore based on factual evidences?
5. How could we use the basic tenants of each religion to lovingly open up a conversation or dialogue with them on the person of Christ?

Here are my top 3 recommended readings for a greater understanding this chapter:

1. *Cross Examination: The Evidence for Belief* by Subodh Pandit (2011)
2. *Beyond Opinion: Living the Faith We Defend* by Ravi Zacharias (2010)
3. *Mere Christianity* by C. S. Lewis (1952)

7

The Entire Biblical Story in a Nutshell

> Christianity provides a unified answer for the whole of life. Each generation of the church in each setting has the responsibility of communicating the gospel in understandable terms, considering the language and thought-forms of that setting.
>
> —Francis A. Schaeffer

Again, this small book cannot do justice to the engrossing story of our history and the purpose of existence found within the pages of the Bible, but what it can do is give you the basics of the entire story that the majority of theologians, historians, and biblical scholars agree to and then simply encourage you to go out and research the details for yourself and share them with others.

Old Testament Books

The Old Testament divides into four major sections that relate to the nation of Israel as God's chosen people from the standpoint of their major characteristics or focus[1]:

1. The Law – Relates to Israel's moral life
2. The historical – Relates to Israel's national development and life
3. The poetical – Relates to Israel's spiritual life

---

1   www.Carm.org

4. The prophetical – Relates to Israel's future life as fulfilled in the Messiah

The Old Testament has thirty-nine books total, with the first five being known as the Torah:

The *Torah*, also known as the Pentateuch, refers to the *five books of the Bible*—the entirety of Judaism's founding legal and ethical religious texts. Outside of its central significance in Judaism, the *Torah* is accepted by Christianity as part of the Bible, comprising the first five books of the Old Testament. The various denominations of Judaism and Christianity hold a diverse spectrum of views regarding the exactitude of the Scripture. As we have mentioned earlier, the Genesis account gives not only the Hebrew creation of the universe and life, it also parallels the vast majority of other creation stories, which make sense if all civilization could be traced back to the same origin. As mentioned earlier, the Torah is the first five books of the Bibles, with Genesis discussing the creation out of nothing by God and then leading into Abraham as the leader of the people later known as the Jewish nation, having a son named Isaac, who in turn had a son named Jacob, who had twelve sons who would become the heads of the twelve tribes of Israel.

Genesis ends with the story of one of these sons—Joseph, who rose to power in Egypt but was forgotten in the generations that followed—leading to the enslavement of the Jewish nation. This slavery led to God raising up Moses and leading his people out of Egypt during the exodus into the desert toward the Promised Land. During this exodus, God provides Moses and the rebellious people with the Ten Commandments and provides direction to the building of a Tabernacle in which God will dwell with them in essence. (This same essence will later be in King Solomon's Temple and ultimately in the Virgin Mary, as the prophets foretold, to be housed in the "Temple of Flesh" so to speak as God Incarnate via Jesus of Nazareth). Many, many things such as Jacob's ladder, the bronze serpent, the manna, the blood on the doorpost during the exodus, the Tabernacle, and the sacrificial high priest structure itself, all standing for a manifestation/representation of this "God Incarnate," are represented throughout the Torah but are far beyond the scope or purpose of this book, which is to serve as simply giving you the basic 101 level tools of understanding the Bible. This book will hopefully serve as a stepping stone to encourage you to read further details on these concepts of theology and other works by authors much more qualified than myself. Just note that the Messiah, Jesus of Nazareth, is represented throughout the Old Hebrew Testament.

Picture of the Ark of the Covenant, where God dwelled in essence/spirit with the Jewish people after the exodus, then was housed in King Solomon's Temple. Eventually the essence/spirit entered the womb of a virgin (Mary), as foretold by the prophets, and came to be housed in the bodily temple known as Jesus of Nazareth, hence the term God Incarnate.

The Law (Torah or Pentateuch)

There are five books total.

- Genesis – Creation; the fall; the Flood; spread of the nations; Abraham, Isaac, Jacob, and Joseph; enslavement in Egypt

- Exodus – Enslavement, Moses, ten plagues, Passover, leaving Egypt, crossing the Red Sea, Mount Sinai, and the Ten Commandments
- Leviticus – Instructions on sacrificial system and the priesthood, instructions on moral purity
- Numbers – Still at Mount Sinai, people making false idol, punishment, forty years' wandering begins
- Deuteronomy – Moses's discourses on God's acts for Israel; the Decalogue; the ceremonial, civil, and social laws; and covenant ratification

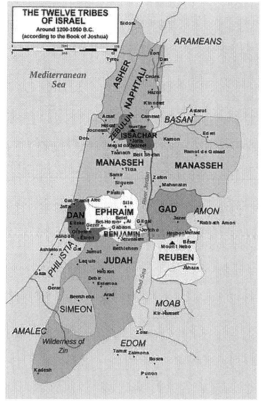

Map of Israel with the twelve tribes shown.

The Historical Books

As previously mentioned, the Old Testament can be divided into four basic sections, with each providing a specific focus with regard to the person of Christ. With Joshua through Esther, we come to the second group of twelve books that deals with the history of the nation of Israel. These books cover the life of the nation from their possession of the land down to the two deportations and loss of the land because of unbelief and disobedience. Covering about eight hundred years of Israel's history, these twelve books tell about the conquering and possession of Canaan, the reigns of the judges, the establishment of kings, the division of Israel into the Northern and Southern Kingdoms, the fall of the Northern Kingdom to Assyria, the exile of the Southern Kingdom into Babylon, and the return to Jerusalem under the leadership of men like Nehemiah and Ezra.

There are twelve books total.

1. Joshua – The first half of Joshua describes the seven-year conquest of the Promised Land; the last half deals with partitioning the lands to the people.
2. Judges – The time of Judges was a bad time period. The Israelites did not drive out all the inhabitants of Canaan and began to take part in their idolatry. There were seven cycles of foreign oppression, repentance, and deliverance. In the end, the people failed to learn their lesson.
3. Ruth – She is a Moabitess known as the kinsman redeemer in Boaz, redeeming Ruth. She speaks of righteousness, love, and faithfulness to the Lord.

The next six books trace the time from Samuel to the captivity.

1. First Samuel – Samuel carries Israel from judges to King Saul.

2. Second Samuel – The people choose a king of their choosing, Saul, eventually replaced by King David.
3. First Kings – Solomon takes the throne after his father David's death. Israel is at its most powerful. Solomon dies, then the division of tribes occur: ten to the north and two to the south.
4. Second Kings – It talks of the divided kingdom. All nineteen kings of Israel were bad. There was captivity in Assyria (722 BC). In Judah, eight of twenty rulers were good but went into exile too (586 BC).
5. First Chronicles – A recounting of the history of Israel to the time of Solomon.
6. Second Chronicles – This is the continued recounting of the life of Solomon, the building of temple, the captivity. It is about the History of Judah only.

The next three books deal with Israel's restoration.

1. Ezra – Cyrus let most of the Jews return to their land of Israel. Zerubbabel led the people (539 BC). Ezra returned later with more Jews (458 BC). Built the temple.
2. Nehemiah – Building the walls of Jerusalem. Nehemiah got permission from the king of Persia to rebuild the walls (444 BC). Revival in the land.
3. Esther – Took place during chapters 6 and 7 of Ezra. Mordecai. Plot to kill the Jewish people.

The Poetical and Wisdom Books

The previous survey of the first seventeen books (Law and history), Genesis through Nehemiah, covered the whole history of the Old Testament. The seventeen books that lie behind us are *historical*. These five poetical books are *experiential*. The seventeen historical books are concerned with a *nation*, as such.

These five poetical books are concerned with *individuals*, as such. The seventeen have to do with *the Hebrew race*. These five have to do with *the human heart*. These five so-called "poetical books" are not the only poetry in the Old Testament Scriptures. We ought clearly to understand, also, that the term "poetical" refers only to their form. It must not be thought to imply that they are simply the product of human imagination. These books portray real human experience, and grapple with profound problems, and express big realities. Especially to their concern themselves with the experiences of the *godly*, in the varying vicissitudes of this changeful life which is ours under the sun …

There are five poetical books.

1. Job – A righteous man tested by God. Deals with God's sovereignty. (Very old book taking place sometime between Noah and Moses.)
2. Psalms – Consists of five divisions. Worship in song. Large variety of subjects.
3. Proverbs – Practical wisdom in everyday affairs.
4. Ecclesiastes – All is vanity. The wisdom of man is futility. As Solomon reflects and hopefully repents on his life of power, wealth, and prosperity; he concludes with the fact that all is vanity except focus on God.
5. Song of Solomon – A song between Solomon and his Shulammite bride, displaying the love between a man and a woman.

The Prophets and Exile

The Prophets of Israel Viewed as a Whole

The first division of the Old Testament was known as the Law, with the second being called the Former Prophets, but these included four books which have already been outlined—Joshua, Judges, Samuel, and Kings. Though these books deal with the history of Israel, they were composed from a prophetic viewpoint, and possibly even the authors themselves may have been prophets by profession.

The seventeen books considered in this section were classified in the Hebrew Bible as the Latter Prophets. The term *latter* speaks primarily of their place in the canon rather than of their chronological position. These prophets are sometimes called *the writing prophets* because their authors wrote or recorded their utterances. There were other *oral prophets* like Nathan, Ahijah, Iddo, Jehu, Elijah, Elisha, Oded, Shemaiah, Azariah, Hanani, Jahaziel, and Huldah, who left no records of their utterances. Mostly because of their size, the Latter Prophets are subdivided into the Major Prophets (Isaiah, Jeremiah, and Ezekiel) and the twelve Minor Prophets, whose writings could all be included in one large scroll: the Twelve-Prophet Book. Daniel, usually viewed as one of the Major Prophets in the English Bible, actually appears in the third division of the Hebrew Canon called the Writings.

Their Directive or Message

As a mouthpiece or spokesman for God, the prophet's primary duty was to speak forth God's message to God's people in the historical context of what was happening among God's people. The broadest meaning is that of *forthtelling*. The narrower meaning is that of *foretelling*. In the process of proclaiming God's message, the prophet would sometimes reveal that which pertained to the future, but contrary to popular opinion, this was only a small part of the prophet's message. *Forthtelling* involved *insight* into the will of God. It was *exhortative*, challenging men to obey. On the other hand, *foretelling* entailed *foresight* into the plan of God. It was *predictive*, either encouraging the righteous in view of God's promises or warning in view of coming judgment. So the prophet was the divinely chosen spokesman who, having received God's message, proclaimed it in oral, visual, or written form to the people. For this reason, a common formula used by the prophets was, "Thus says the Lord." As God's spokesmen, their message can be seen in a threefold function they had among the people of God in the Old Testament:

First, they functioned as preachers. They expounded and interpreted the Mosaic Law to the nation. It was their duty to admonish, reprove, denounce sin, threaten with the terrors of judgment, call to repentance, and bring consolation and pardon. Their activity of rebuking sin and calling for repentance consumed far more of the prophets' time than any other feature of their work.

Second, they functioned as predictors. They announced the coming judgment, deliverance, and events relating to the Messiah and His kingdom. Predicting the future was never intended merely to satisfy man's curiosity but was designed to demonstrate that God knows and controls the future and to give purposeful revelation. The prediction given by a true prophet would be visibly fulfilled. The failure of the prediction to be fulfilled would indicate that the prophet had not spoken the word of *Yahweh* (cf. Deut. 18:20–22).

Finally, they functioned as watchmen over the people of Israel. Ezekiel stood as a watchman on the walls of Zion, ready to trumpet a warning against religious apostasy (Ezek. 3:17). He warned the people against political and military alliances with foreign powers, the temptation to become involved in idolatry and Canaanite cultic worship and the danger of placing excessive confidence in religious formalism and sacrificial ritual.

While the prophets functioned in various ways as they communicated God's message, they occupied *one major role* in Israel's religious system. The prophets in Israel occupied the role of *a royal diplomat* or *prosecuting attorney*, indicting the nation for violations of the Mosaic covenant.

There are seventeen prophetical books.

There are five books about the Major Prophets:

1. Isaiah – Looks at the sin of Judah and proclaims God's judgment. Coming restoration and blessing.

2. Jeremiah – Called by God to proclaim the news of judgment to Judah, which came. God establishes a New Covenant. Foretells of the Messiah who will put God's law in their hearts.
3. Lamentations – Five poems of lament. Description of defeat and fall of Jerusalem by Jeremiah.
4. Ezekiel – He ministered to the Jews in captivity in Babylon. Description of the end of times.
5. Daniel – Many visions of the future for the Gentiles and the Jews.

There are twelve books on the Minor Prophets:

1. Hosea – Story of Hosea and his unfaithful wife, Gomer. Represents God's love and faithfulness and Israel's spiritual adultery. Israel will be judged and restored.
2. Joel – Proclaims a terrifying future using the imagery of locusts. Judgment will come, but blessing will follow.
3. Amos – He warned Israel of its coming judgment. Israel rejects God's warning. Focus on social reform.
4. Obadiah – A proclamation against Edom, a neighboring nation of Israel that gloated over Jerusalem's judgments. Prophecy of its utter destruction.
5. Jonah – Jonah proclaims a coming judgment upon Nineveh's people. They repented, and judgment was spared.
6. Micah – Description of the complete moral decay in all levels of Israel. God will judge but will forgive and restore.
7. Nahum – Nineveh has gone into apostasy (approximately 125 years after Jonah) and will be destroyed.
8. Habakkuk – Near the end of the kingdom of Judah, Habakkuk asks God why He is not dealing with Judah's

sins. God says He will use the Babylonians.. Habakkuk asks how God can use a nation that is even worse than Judah.

9. Zephaniah – The theme is developed of the Day of the Lord and His judgment with a coming blessing. Judah will not repent, except for a remnant, which will be restored.
10. Haggai – The people failed to put God first by building their houses before they finished God's temple; therefore, they had no prosperity.
11. Zechariah – Zechariah encourages the Jews to complete the temple. There are many messianic prophecies.
12. Malachi – God's people are lax in their duty to God, resulting in a growing distance from God. There is moral compromise and the proclamation of the coming judgment.

The Intertestamental Period (Between Old and New Testaments)

I would not say that a knowledge of the period between the Old and New Testaments is vital to one's understanding of the four Gospels, but it is very desirable and indeed quite necessary if we would fully appreciate many of the scenes and incidents on which Matthew lifts the curtain. It gives a background against which we see with clearness the connections and relevance of the sayings and doings that occupy the earlier pages of our New Testament.

The Period in General

With the Old Testament canon closing with Malachi at about 397 BC, we see that this period between Malachi and Matthew covers some four hundred years. This four-hundred-year interval has been called the dark or silent period of Israel's history in pre-Christian times because during it, there was neither prophet nor inspired writer. With this period, we seem to find the sad fulfillment of Psalm 74:9 (KJV) upon Israel: "We see not our signs; there is no more any prophet; neither is there among us any that knoweth how long."

The condition of the Jews as a nation and race at the beginning of this four-hundred-year period should be kept in mind. Two hundred years earlier, Jerusalem had been overthrown and the Jewish people carried into the Babylonian exile (606 BC–586 BC) as punishment for their unfaithfulness to God. At the end of this seventy-year punishment period, the Babylonian empire was already overthrown and succeeded by that of Media-Persia (536 BC). Cyrus, the Persian emperor, issued a decree permitting the return of the Jews to Israel. Under the leadership of Zerubbabel, some five thousand Jews returned. Some twenty years after their return, after many setbacks, the building of the Temple was completed in 516 BC. Then after another fifty-eight years had passed, in 458 BC, Ezra, the scribe, returned to Jerusalem with a small group of Israelites and restored the Law and the ritual. Still another thirteen years later, in 445 BC, Nehemiah had come to Jerusalem to rebuild the walls and become governor. Now once again, there was a Jewish state in Judea, though of course under Persian rule.

Such is the picture of the Jewish people at the beginning of the four-hundred-year period between Malachi and Matthew: the Jewish remnant back in Judea for about one hundred and forty years (536 BC–397 BC), a small dependent Jewish state there, Jerusalem and the temple rebuilt, the Law and the ritual restored but with the mass of the people remaining dispersed throughout the Medo-Persian empire. This eventually led to the Greek conquest by Alexander the Great and the introduction of Greek culture throughout Israel. This also led to the formation of the Hasmoean Dynasty, which is described in the Apocryphal books of Maccabees that introduced groups such as the Pharisees and Sadducees of Jesus's time and set up the eventual place of

Roman rule, which endorsed King Herod. This is the point "in the fullness of time" that Jesus enters into human history.

The New Testament

Picture of Rylands Library Papyrus P52 (Gospel of John dated to 125 AD). There are over 5,750 Greek New Testament manuscripts, and counting Latin, Coptic, Syrian, etc., there are over 20,000 all matching to an accuracy on all major points to over 99 percent the same when compared with today's New Testament. This has warranted the New Testament to be deemed the most accurate ancient literature in human history, written the closest to the actual time of the events, with the highest number of manuscript support than any other piece of ancient literature.

The New Testament is a record of historical events, the Good News events of the saving life of the Lord Jesus Christ—His life, death, resurrection, ascension, and the continuation of His work in the world—which is explained and applied by the apostles whom He chose and sent into the world. It is also the fulfillment of those events long anticipated by the Old Testament. Further, it is sacred history, which, unlike secular history, was written under the supernatural guidance of the Holy Spirit. This means it, like the Old Testament, possesses divine authority for us today and throughout human history until the Lord Himself returns.

Origin and Meaning of the Term *New Testament*

Our Bible is divided into two sections we call the Old Testament and the New Testament, but exactly what does that mean? The Greek word for *testament, diaqhkh* (in Latin, *testamentum*), means "will," "testament," or "covenant." But as used in connection with the New Testament, "covenant" is the best translation. As such, it refers to a new arrangement made by one party into which others could enter if they accepted the covenant. As used of God's covenants, it designates a new relationship into which men may be received by God. The Old Testament or covenant is primarily a record of God's dealings with the Israelites on the basis of the Mosaic Covenant given at Mount Sinai. On the other hand, the New Testament or covenant (anticipated in Jeremiah 31:31 and instituted by the Lord Jesus in 1 Corinthians 11:25) describes the new arrangement of God with men from every tribe and tongue and people and nation who will accept salvation on the basis of grace through Christ.

The old covenant revealed the holiness of God in the righteous standard of the law and promised a coming Redeemer. The new covenant shows the holiness of God in His righteous Son. The New Testament then contains those writings that reveal the content of this new covenant. The message of the New Testament centers on (1) the person who gave Himself for the remission of sins (Matt. 26:28) and (2) the people (the community of believers which is much more different than the church we think of today in institutionalized forms) who have received His salvation. Thus the central theme of the New Testament is salvation. The names *Old* and *New Covenants* were thus applied first to the two relationships into which God entered with men, and then to the books that contained the record of these two relationships. The New Testament is the divine treaty by the terms of which God has received us rebels and enemies into peace with himself.

Divine Preparation for the New Testament

In the time of the New Testament, Rome was the dominant world power and ruled over most of the ancient world. Yet in a small town in Palestine, in Bethlehem of Judea, was born one who would change the world. Concerning this person, the apostle Paul wrote, "But when the fullness of the time came, God sent forth His Son, born of a woman, born under the Law [i.e., the Old Covenant]" (Gal. 4:4, NASB). In several special and wonderful ways, God had prepared the world for the coming of Messiah. Several factors contributed to this preparation.

Preparation through the Jewish Nation

The preparation for the coming of Christ is the story of the Old Testament. The Jews were chosen of God from all the nations to be a treasured possession as a kingdom of priests and a holy nation (Exod. 1:5–6). In that regard, it began with the promises of God given to the patriarchs, Abraham, Isaac, and Jacob (Gen. 12:1–3, Rom. 9:4). They were to be the custodians of God's Word or the Old Testament (Rom. 3:2) and the channel of the Redeemer (Gen. 12:3, Gal. 3:8, Rom. 9:5). The Old Testament, therefore, was full of Christ and anticipated His coming as a suffering and glorified Savior. Furthermore, these prophesies were not only many but very precise, giving details of Messiah's lineage, place of birth, and the conditions around the time of His birth, life, death, and even His resurrection.

Though Israel was disobedient and was taken into captivity as God's judgment for her hardness of heart, God nevertheless brought a remnant back to their homeland after seventy years as He had promised in preparation for the coming of the Messiah. Though four hundred years had passed after the writing of the last Old Testament book and though the religious climate was one of Pharisaic externalism and hypocrisy, there was a spirit of messianic anticipation in the air, and a remnant was looking for the Messiah.

James Stroud

The Collection of the Books of the New Testament

As we alluded to in chapter 5, originally, the books of the New Testament were separately circulated and only gradually collected together to form what we now know as the New Testament part of the canon of Scripture. By preservation of God, our twenty-seven New Testament books were set apart from many other writings during the early church. They were preserved as a part of the New Testament canon because of their inspiration and apostolic authority. After they were written, the individual books were not immediately gathered together into the canon or collection of twenty-seven that comprise the New Testament. Groups of books like Paul's letters and the Gospels were preserved at first by the body of believers to whom they were sent, and gradually, all twenty-seven books were collected and formally acknowledged by the church as a whole. This majority of the New Testament was in circulation approximately AD 150, with the majority of ancient writings (such as the Muratorian Canon) we have agreeing to the books of the New Testament. In the second century, the circulation of books that promoted heresy accentuated the need for distinguishing valid Scripture from other Christian literature. Certain tests were developed to determine which books should be included.

1. Was the book written or approved by an apostle?
2. Were its contents of a spiritual nature?
3. Did it give evidence of being inspired by God?
4. Was it widely received by the body of believers (ecclesia)?

Not all of the twenty-seven books that were eventually recognized as canonical were accepted by all the churches in the early centuries, but this does not mean that those that were not immediately or universally accepted were spurious. Letters addressed to individuals (Philemon, 2 and 3 John) would not have been circulated as widely as those sent to churches. The books most disputed were James, Jude, 2 Peter, 2 and 3 John, and Philemon, but ultimately these were included, and the canon was certified at the Council of Carthage in AD 397.

New Testament Books

The New Testament has 27 books total, which consist of the following:

- Historical books – Matthew, Mark, Luke, John, Acts
- Pauline Epistles – Romans, 1 Corinthians, 2 Corinthians, Galatians, Ephesians, Philippians, Colossians, 1 Thessalonians, 2 Thessalonians, 1 Timothy, 2 Timothy, Titus, Philemon
- Non-Pauline Epistles – Hebrews, James, 1 Peter, 2 Peter, 1 John, 2 John, 3 John, Jude, Revelation

Historical Books: The Gospels and Early Church

1. Matthew – Presents Jesus as the Messiah. Genealogy of Jesus through Joseph. Fulfillment of OT prophecy. (Written by Matthew, the apostle of Jesus.)

2. Mark – Presents Jesus as the servant. One-third of the gospel deals with the last week of His life. Generally agreed to be the first written Gospel. (Mark was a follower of Peter, the apostle.)

3. Luke – Presents Jesus as the Son of Man to seek and save the lost. Genealogy of Jesus through Mary. Largest of the Gospels.

4. John – Presents Jesus as God in flesh, the Christ, so that you might believe. Written by John, the apostle, the only apostle not to be martyred (also penned Revelations).

5. Acts – Historical account from Jesus's ascension to travels of Paul in his missionary journeys. This was originally a two-part document with the Gospel of Luke (Luke wrote both of them). This gives an early history of the church (ecclesia), its body of believers, and how the church got started (and how it is different than the institutionalized church today).

Pauline Epistles

1. Romans – A systematic examination of justification, sanctification, and glorification. Examines God's plan for the Jews and the Gentiles.
2. 1 Corinthians – This letter deals with factions and corrections due to immorality, lawsuits, and abuse of the Lord's Supper. Also mentions idols, marriage, and the resurrection.
3. 2 Corinthians – Paul's defense of his apostolic position.
4. Galatians – Paul refutes the errors of legalism and examines the proper place of grace in the Christian's life.
5. Ephesians – The believer's position in Christ and information on spiritual warfare.
6. Philippians – Paul speaks of his imprisonment and his love for the Philippians. He exhorts them to godliness and warns them of legalism.
7. Colossians – Paul focuses on the preeminence of Jesus in creation, redemption, and godliness.
8. 1 Thessalonians – Paul's ministry to the Thessalonians. Teachings on purity and mentions the return of Christ.
9. 2 Thessalonians – Corrections on the Day of the Lord.
10. 1 Timothy – Instructions to Timothy on proper leadership and dealings with false teachers, the role of women, prayer, and requirements of elders and deacons.

11. 2 Timothy – A letter of encouragement to Timothy to be strong.
12. Titus – Paul left Titus in Crete to care for the churches there. Requirements for elders.
13. Philemon – A letter to the owner of a runaway slave. Paul appeals to Philemon to forgive Onesimus.

Non-Pauline Epistles

1. Hebrews – A letter to the Hebrew Christians in danger of returning to Judaism. It demonstrates the superiority of Jesus over the OT system. Mentions the Melchizedek priesthood. (Hebrews may be of Pauline origin. There is much debate on its authorship).
2. James – a practical exhortation of believers to live a Christian life evidencing regeneration. It urges self-examination of the evidence of the changed life.
3. 1 Peter – Peter wrote this letter to encourage its recipients in the light of their suffering and to be humble in it. It mentions baptism.
4. 2 Peter – This deals with the person on an inward level. It has warnings against false teachers and mentions the Day of the Lord.
5. 1 John – John describes true fellowship of the believers with other believers and with God. Describes God as light and love. Encourages a holy Christian walk before the Lord. Much mention of Christian love.
6. 2 John – Praise for walking in Christ and a reminder to walk in God's love.
7. 3 John – John thanks Gaius for his kindness to God's people and rebukes Diotrephes.
8. Jude – Exposes false teachers and uses OT allusions to demonstrate the judgment upon them. Contends for the faith.

9. Revelation – A highly symbolic vision of the future rebellion, judgment, and consummation of all things.

Thanks to partners at http://carm.org/Matt Slick for providing parts of the Old and New Testament breakdown.

You should be able to answer these questions after reading this chapter:

1. What is the Old Testament versus the New Testament (in a nutshell if someone asked)?
2. Who were the Patriarchs and the Prophets and what role did they play?
3. Briefly describe the period of the Judges versus that of the Davidic monarchy. What were the differences?
4. Why did the monarchy fall? When was Israel conquered and by whom? When was Judah conquered and by whom?
5. What happened between the Old and New Testaments?
6. What is the "Good News" if someone asked you?
7. Based on the Book of Acts, do you feel that your church closely follows the early church? Why or why not?

Here are my top 3 recommended readings for a greater understanding this chapter:

1. *Encountering the Old Testament: A Christian Survey (Encountering Biblical Studies)* by Bill T. Arnold and Bryan E. Beyer (2008)
2. *Encountering the New Testament: A Historical and Theological Survey (Encountering Biblical Studies)* by Walter A. Elwell and Robert W. Yarbrough (2005)
3. *The Philosophy of History: Naturalism and* Religion by James Stroud (2013)

8

Main Events in Biblical History

> Christianity is the only worldview that adequately answers all questions asked by reality itself. Other religions are not founded in history. The Bible claims to be rooted in history; both Old and New Testaments. It is insisted upon as real history which makes it quite unique among all worldviews.
>
> —Francis A. Schaeffer

This time line is referenced from http://www.bible-history.com.

Note that approximate biblical dating follows scholarship consensus. Some dates are uncertain, and all are approximate dating, with many scholars differing +/- five years. There is also some overlap in the case of the judges and the kings, but this should help you to get a better grasp of when the events of the Bible (Old and New Testaments) took place and of their historic setting as described in the book.

BC

- 2090 BC – Abraham called by God.
- 2067 – Isaac is born.
- 2007 – Jacob is born.
- 1992 – Abraham dies.
- 1944 – Isaac dies.
- 1877 – Jacob arrives in Egypt.
- 1860 – Jacob dies in Egypt.
- 1806 – Joseph dies in Egypt.

- 1730 – Hyksos' invasion of Egypt. Hebrews bondage begins.
- 1548 – Hebrew midwives ordered to destroy all Hebrew male children
- 1528 – All newborn Hebrew males are to be cast into the Nile.
- 1525 – Moses is born.
- 1487 – Moses flees Egypt.
- 1483 – The great oppression of the Hebrews begins.
- 1447 – The Exodus begins.
- 1446 – The Tabernacle is constructed.
- 1407 – Moses dies. Joshua conquers Canaan.
- 1400 – The conquest of Canaan is completed.
- 1375 – Othniel becomes a judge.
- 1319 – Ehud becomes a judge.
- 1318 – Rameses I founds the nineteenth dynasty in Egypt.
- 1240 – Deborah and Barak judge Israel.
- 1194 – Gideon becomes a judge.
- 1167 – Eli is born.
- 1155 – Abimelech usurps power in Israel.
- 1152 – Tola becomes a judge.
- 1131 – Jair becomes a judge.
- 1109 – Eli becomes a priest.
- 1105 – Samuel is born.
- 1089 – Jephthah becomes a judge.
- 1083 – Ibzan becomes a judge.
- 1071 – Elon becomes a judge. Samson becomes judge.

- 1069 – Samuel begins to minister.
- 1066 – Abdon becomes a judge (last of the judges).
- 1043 – Saul becomes a king.
- 1011 – Saul and Jonathan are slain; David becomes king of Judah.
- 1004 – David becomes king over all Israel.
- 971 – Solomon ascends the throne.
- 966 – Solomon begins to build the Temple in Jerusalem.
- 931 – Rehoboam becomes king of Israel and Judah.
- 931 – Jeroboam rebels, sets up a rival kingdom in the north (this causes Israel to be split into two separate kingdoms known as Judah and Israel).
- 913 – Abijam becomes king of Judah.
- 911 – Asa becomes king of Judah.
- 910 – Nadab becomes king of Israel.
- 909 – Bausha becomes king of Israel.
- 886 – Elah becomes king of Israel. Zimri becomes king of Israel.
- 885 – Tibni becomes king of Israel.
- 880 – Omri becomes king of Israel.
- 874 – Ahab becomes king of Israel.
- 873 – Jehoshaphat becomes king of Judah.
- 858 – Elijah begins to prophesy.
- 853 – Ahaziah becomes king of Israel.
- 853 – Jehoram becomes king of Judah.
- 852 – Joram becomes king of Israel.
- 852 – Elisha begins to prophesy.

- 841 – Jehu becomes king of Israel.
- 841 – Ahaziah becomes king of Judah.
- 841 – Athaliah seizes the throne of Judah.
- 835 – Joash becomes king of Judah.
- 830 – Joel prophesies.
- 814 – Jehoahaz becomes king of Israel.
- 798 – Jehoash becomes king of Israel.
- 796 – Amaziah becomes king of Judah.
- 790 – Uzziah becomes coregent of Judah.
- 783 – Jonah begins his ministry.
- 782 – Jeroboam II becomes king of Israel.
- 767 – Uzziah becomes full king of Judah.
- 764 – Amos begins to prophesy.
- 755 – Hosea begins to prophesy.
- 753 – Rome founded. Zechariah becomes king of Israel.
- 752 – Shallum becomes king of Israel.
- 752 – Menahem becomes king of Israel.
- 742 – Pekahiah becomes king of Israel.
- 740 – Pekah becomes king of Israel.
- 739 – Uzziah dies. Isaiah begins to prophesy.
- 739 – Jotham becomes king of Judah.
- 736 – Micah begins to prophesy.
- 735 – Ahaz becomes king of Judah.
- 732 – Hoshea becomes king of Israel.
- 722 – Sargon II becomes king of Assyria. Samaria falls.
- 722 – The ten tribes of Israel go into captivity.

- 715 – Hezekiah becomes king of Judah.
- 701 – Judah is invaded by the Assyrians.
- 686 – Manasseh becomes king of Judah.
- 648 – Nahum predicts the fall of Nineveh.
- 642 – Amon becomes king of Judah.
- 640 – Josiah becomes king of Judah.
- 634 – Zephaniah begins to prophesy.
- 627 – Jeremiah begins to prophesy.
- 622 – Revival occurs in Judah.
- 619 – Habakkuk begins to prophesy.
- 612 – Nineveh falls.
- 609 – Neco II becomes pharaoh of Egypt.
- 609 – Jehoahaz becomes king of Judah.
- 609 – Jehoiakim becomes king of Judah.
- 605 – Nebuchadnezzar becomes king of Babylon.
- 605 – The Babylonians invade Judah. Daniel begins to prophesy.
- 597 – Jehoachin becomes king of Judah.
- 597 – Zedekiah becomes king of Judah.
- 593 – Ezekiel begins to prophesy.
- 586 – The Babylonians destroy Jerusalem and the Temple.
- 586 – The Jews are deported to Babylon.
- 550 – Cyrus becomes king of Persia.
- 539 – Babylon falls to the Medes and Persians.
- 538 – Zerubbabel and Joshua lead a small party back to Palestine.
- 536 – The Second Temple is started in Jerusalem.

- 520 – Zechariah begins to prophesy.
- 520 – Haggai begins to prophesy.
- 520 – Construction of the Jerusalem Temple is resumed.
- 516 – The Temple is completed.
- 509 – The Roman Republic is founded.
- 478 – Esther becomes queen of Persia.
- 478 – Esther saves the Jews of the empire from extermination.
- 458 – Ezra takes a small contingent of Jews back to Palestine.
- 445 – Nehemiah takes a small contingent of Jews back to Palestine.
- 443 – Nehemiah and Ezra read the Scriptures to the Jews.
- 436 – Malachi begins to prophesy.
- 332 – The Greek ruler Alexander the Great destroys the Persian Empire and gains control over Judea (Israel).
- 168 – (1–2 Maccabees) Antiochus pollutes the Temple in Jerusalem and suspends the sacrifices of the Jews.
- 166 – Matthias leads the Jews in revolt against Antiochus Epiphanes.
- 165 – The Jerusalem Temple is repaired and cleansed.
- 63 – The Romans conquer the Greek (Seleucid) Empire and gain control of Judea (Israel).
- 40 – Herod is appointed king.
- 37 – Herod captures Jerusalem.
- 20 – Herod begins to rebuild the Jerusalem Temple.
- 4 – Herod dies.
- 4 – The birth of Jesus.

AD

- AD 14 – Augustus Caesar dies, and Tiberius becomes Roman emperor.
- 26 – Jesus begins to teach. He characterizes rabbinic teaching (the Mishna) as vain tradition.
- 30 – Jesus is crucified and raised from the dead.
- 30 – Full Pentecost. The Christian church is born.
- 54 – Nero becomes Roman emperor.
- 59 – The apostle Paul is imprisoned at Caesarea.
- 60 – Paul appears before Agrippa.
- 61 – Paul becomes a prisoner at Rome.
- 66 – The Jews of Judea revolt against Rome.
- 68 – Paul is martyred at Rome.
- 69 – Jerusalem is besieged by the Romans.
- 70 – Jerusalem falls. The Temple burned. The Jews are deported.

Conclusion

> Public School Education is thus a most powerful ally of humanism. What can a theistic Sunday school's meeting for an hour once a week and teaching only a fraction of the children do to stem the tide of the five-day program of humanistic (public school) teaching?
>
> —*Humanism: A New Religion*, 1930

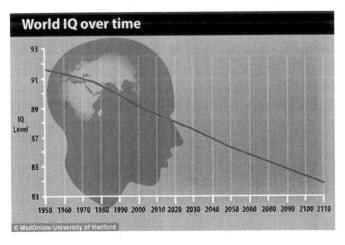

Some people have asked me if teaching these types of truths might lessen a student's knowledge level since evolutionists/naturalists have collectively labeled Christian theists/creationists as nonintellectual. Interestingly enough, an article from a secular educational research company recently discovered that the largest Protestant-Christian educational system (Seventh-day Adventist, of which I am not affiliated with) scored higher than the much heavier tax-funded public school systems in every field of testing.

Not only does the Seventh-day Adventist educational system endorse a literal six-day creation of Genesis as well as a recent creation, they are simple and have only a fraction of money to work with compared to the secular school systems, and yet they scored higher in every field of testing including science. I think this is a fitting article to conclude this book with:

Elissa Kiddo, EdD, professor of curriculum and instruction at La Sierra University, relates some findings from the Cognitive-Genesis research project she directs.

> Between 2006 and 2010, my colleagues and I analyzed test scores of 51,706 students, based on the Iowa Test of Basic Skills for Grades 3-8, the Iowa Test of Educational Development for Grades 9 and 11, and the Cognitive Abilities Test for all grades, as well as surveys completed by students, parents, teachers, and school administrators. In each subject category, students attending Adventist schools scored higher than the national average. They also scored higher than their expected achievement based on assessment of individual ability – a factor few other schools measure. One of our most dramatic findings is that students who transferred to Adventist schools saw a marked improvement in academic achievement. The more years a student attended an Adventist school, the more his or her performance improved.[1]

The study also reports that socioeconomic status and funding are not factors. In fact, according to "research by Dave Lawrence, a graduate student at La Sierra University...students at Adventist schools that spend as little as $2,000 to $4,000 per pupil are roughly at the same achievement level as students in schools

---

[1] "Study Shows that Adventist Education Improves Learning," last modified November 19, 2010, http://spectrummagazine.org/article/alexander-carpenter/2010/11/19/study-shows-adventist-education-improves-learning.

that spend as much as $12,000 per student. Mr. Lawrence found no significant correlation between a school's budget and student achievement." The piece suggests that the cause is the holistic philosophy of Adventist education, with its emphasis on the mental, spiritual, and the physical. Similar to this article (which I used since it was from a secular source), the majority of private schools and homeschools score on average 25–35 percent higher in all areas of education than do public schools. Public schools (which I attended) have unfortunately drifted away from educating children to focusing more on socializing and pushing politically correct agendas upon them, and this is why I highly encourage any parents out there to investigate private schools and homeschooling. I know it is not always easy, but I believe well worth it for our children's future, as well as for their ability to take the evidence where it leads.

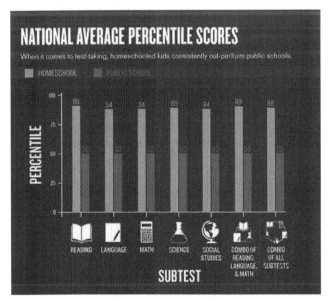

From http://infographicjournal.com/homeschool-domination/.

My hope is that this simple book will at least encourage you to better understand what it means to be a disciple of Christ, to at least understand the message in the context of what C. S. Lewis called "mere Christianity" in its simplest form, to share that simplicity with others, to research the information yourself, and, if you are not a follower of Christ, to at least consider it. (Do not be dissuaded by "church-ianity" versus Christ-ianity if you have been hurt or offended by the actions of those who claim to be His followers because in the end, this is not a valid excuse for not following Christ.) I would also strongly suggest you find a good biblical church (though they are becoming harder to find they are out there) and be baptized. Find a good Bible study group and start growing in your new life. These things are important and cannot be taken for granted.

Richard Wurmbrand was a Romanian pastor and founder of Voice of the Martyrs (www.persecution.com). He was forced to serve fourteen years in Communist prisons for being a noncompromising Christian. He wrote of one of the tools that the Soviet Union used to attack Christianity:

> Wherever people know how to write, they have a holy book. Atheists, too, have one – it is called *The Atheist's Handbook*. It was first issued in 1961 by Moscow's Academy of Science. From the primary grades through college, on radio and television, in films and at atheistic rallies, the ideas contained in this book are propagated. In all the Christian countries of the West, atheism has full liberty for its propaganda. Christianity has not the slightest reason to fear it. In free debate, only Christianity can win. Christians have not feared prisons nor the implements of torture. Neither do we fear atheist books. In the struggle of ideas, the final victory can only be ours.[2]

May we all remember this. Our day is not that different than the one Wurmbrand describes above, but compromise is not the

---

2   Richard Wurmbrand, *The Answer to the Atheist's Handbook* (1993), 5–8.

answer. Instead, we must prepare now to show ourselves true and faithful, and as Wurmbrand describes, Christians have nothing to fear. In open debate, Christianity has the answers, and we do not need to be shy or ashamed in telling the world this.

> Draw near to God and He will draw near to you.
> —James 4:8 (NASB)

Afterword

The Lollards were a group of Christian followers who worked with philosopher/theologian John Wycliffe (1385) in translating the first copies of the Bible into English. They went out in pairs of two with a handwritten New Testament and conversed with the public on apologetic concepts as well as philosophical concepts on why Christian theism is the most logical worldview and what the Christian story is all about. They were heavily persecuted by the organized church of the day, but they persevered in order to share the Good News of Jesus Christ of Nazareth. What is our excuse for not doing likewise today?

Since I have kept this book less than 200 pages long, it has only given you the basic facts about Christian theism and what it means. On a good note, because this simple book only touches on subjects at a relatively macro level, it is easy to read and digest, as well as hopefully share with others; moreover, we have not touched on any fine-line topics of theology or church doctrine, so that one can use the information in this book whether they are of Protestant, Anabaptist, Anglican, Roman Catholic, Eastern Orthodox, or people who simply have skeptical mind-sets. The key, in my humble opinion, is that we must not be afraid to engage schools, colleges, universities, churches, and friends with this type information in loving ways, communicating the facts as well as the Good News. Communicating the Good News is going to get more and more difficult in our post-Christian culture, I am afraid. Even secular publications such as the September/October issue of *Biblical Archaeology Review*, which is not a pro-Christian publication by any means, commented in an article titled "Is Bible a Dirty Word?" that many persons are now refusing to submit to their publication due to them still using the word *bible* in their title. Since the word *bible* offends many in our day of socio-relativism and political correctness, many publications are dropping it all together and, in some instances, falsifying their data if it offers too much support to the Bible.

We must never look to apologetics, however, as any type of substitute for the more important part of the moving of God's Spirit in our lives, our personal time with him through prayer and study, and simply experiencing him every day. But if someone asks, "Why are you a Christian," then we need to be able to adequately give them an answer. I have worked in New York City as well as small towns, and having worked with people of other faiths, colleges, and universities and can confirm that if you can digest the basics of this book and communicate them to others in a loving way, the seed will be planted for others to water as God grows. The school systems have practically been handicapped to only hear one side of the evidence (the atheistic/naturalistic view). It is our loving and humble job to ensure they hear the other side. Please let me know if I can be of any assistance at all, and I pray that I do not read any future statistics on Christian ignorance such as these when we have all the tools at our disposal:

> Many high school seniors believe that Sodom and Gomorrah were husband and wife, while a majority of Americans

cannot name one of the four Gospels. Jay Leno asked his Tonight Show audience one night to name one of Jesus' twelve apostles; they came up empty. One in ten Americans believes that Joan of Arc was Noah's wife, and only one-third knows that Jesus (not Billy Graham) preached the Sermon on the Mount. (*Washington Monthly*)

Lord willing, our small museum will be up and running in Northwest Arkansas in 2016, so check back periodically, and we hope to see you in the future.

God be with us all,
James Stroud
www.NWABibleMuseum.org
www.TheLollards.org

In your hearts revere Christ as Lord. Always be prepared to give an answer to everyone who asks you to give the reason for the hope that you have. But do this with gentleness and respect.

—1 Peter 3:15

Appendix
Young Earth Creationism

> The young-earth solution to reconciling the order of creation with natural history makes good exegetical and theological sense. Indeed, the overwhelming consensus of theologians up through the Reformation held to this view. I myself would adopt it in a heartbeat except that nature seems to present such a strong evidence against it. I'm hardly alone in my reluctance to accept young-earth creationism.
>
> —William A. Dembski,
> *The End of Christianity*

Renowned Christian historian Gary Habermas, whom I have had the privilege to visit with, has oftentimes commented, "I am a young-earth creationist about three days out of the week and an old earth-creationist the other four days," which tells you that the topic is hardly solved or one-sided despite what some (such as William Lane Craig) may assert.

During the last three years since the first publication of my work on *The Philosophy of History*, I have been asked about young earth creationism by a variety of sources. Though I fall more into the Francis Schaeffer camp on the subject (agnostic), I have and do go on record as stating unapologetically that what I call recent creation is a much more credible and plausible worldview than any facet of naturalism. Obviously, the flow of my book does take the most up-to-date interpretation of the data (for example, that the universe is approximately 13.7 billion years old), but obviously any dating such as this is problematic and based on many assumptions. Moreover, if naturalism is false and God exists, then I would assume God could create a universe any age he wanted since God is infinite and we are finite, and most (as the quote by Dembski above acknowledges) exegetes recognize that a recent creation seems to make more biblical sense than an ancient one of "billions of years."

After all, I know of no theologian who argues that Adam was created a baby, and even those such as William Lane Craig (who I have worked with) insist we "follow modern-day cosmology" was quite quick to say we "jettison" modern biology when it conflicts with key doctrine such as the virgin birth. (This was after Dr. Craig had said young earth creationism was an "embarrassment" and that if God created a universe that looked old, he would be a deceiver. I then asked if he was a deceiver since modern biology tells us that virgins do not give birth to children as Mary did with Jesus. He did not answer, showing his inconsistency in picking/choosing the data he prefers it would seem.) My point is that one cannot have his cake and eat it too as Dr. Craig oftentimes likes to do. (Keep in mind that I have the highest respect for Dr. Craig as I have operated a philosophy chapter through him for some time. My point is simply that things are not always as black and white as Dr. Craig sometimes suggests (and he knows this.) From my vantage point as a historian, I do find it ironic that history literally does start roughly 4000 BC, and we historians simply know little to nothing before about 3000 BC.

Now this does not mean I am endorsing a 4004 BC midnight creation (some YEC such as Paul Nelson admits the creation could have been 50,000 years ago), I am simply saying there is some plausibility to this, and as the famous systematic theologian Wayne Grudem points out, it does make more sense from a strict biblical/theological/historical standpoint. Therefore instead of me attempting to answer some questions about what recent creation is and is not, I visited Ken Ham, who is probably the biggest name in the YEC movement, and have attached a summation of their position (thanks/citation: www.AnswersInGenesis.org). Like I said, I do not know how old creation is (nor does anyone), and the line of my arguments in this book would apply to a universe created 13.7 billion years ago just as well as it would to one created 10,000 years ago. I am just saying that we cannot dismiss it *a priori*, and it definitely is much more logically plausible than *any* definition of naturalism as I have outlined; therefore, before we cast stones, we should hear from the source itself:

> Young-Earth Creationist View Summarized and Defended
> By Dr. Terry Mortenson on February 16, 2011
>
> Abstract
>
> There is a great amount of controversy in the church today regarding evolution and the age of the earth. Many competing views attract the attention of Christians producing great confusion and leading many Christians to conclude that it just doesn't matter. In this article, I will explain and give a brief defense of the young-earth creationist view as the only proper understanding of Scripture. All other views are compromise with error. I will also explain some of the reasons why this matters for all Christians. This article is an extract from the beginning of a longer paper which was originally published in Answers Research Journal in 2009 as Systematic Theology Texts and the Age of the Earth.
>
> Young-earth creationists believe that the creation days of Genesis 1 were six literal (24-hour) days, which occurred [6,000–12,000] years ago. They believe that about [2,300–4,300] years before Christ, the surface of the earth was radically rearranged by Noah's Flood. All land animals and birds not in Noah's Ark (along with many sea creatures) perished, many of which were subsequently buried in the Flood sediments. Therefore, creationists believe that the global, catastrophic Flood was responsible for most (but not all) of the rock layers and fossils (i.e., some rock layers

and possibly some fossils were deposited before the Flood, while other layers and fossils were produced in postdiluvian localized catastrophic sedimentation events or processes).

The biblical arguments in support of this view can be briefly summarized as follows:

1. Genesis is history, not poetry, parable, prophetic vision, or mythology. This is seen in the Hebrew verbs used in Genesis 1, the fact that Genesis 1–11 has the same characteristics of historical narrative as in Genesis 12–50, most of Exodus, much of Numbers, Joshua, 1 and 2 Kings, etc. (which are discernibly distinct from the characteristics of Hebrew poetry, parable, or prophetic vision), and the way the other biblical authors and Jesus treat Genesis 1–11 (as literal history).

2. The very dominant meaning of yôm in the Old Testament is a literal day, and the context of Genesis 1 confirms that meaning there. Yôm is defined in its two literal senses in verse 5. It is repeatedly used with a number (one day, second day, etc.) and with evening and morning, which elsewhere in the OT always means a literal day. It is defined again literally in verse 14 in relation to the movement of the heavenly bodies.

3. God created the first animate and inanimate things supernaturally and instantly. They were fully formed and fully functioning. For example, plants, animals, and people were mature adults ready to reproduce naturally "after their kinds." When God said "let there be..." He did not have to wait millions of years for things to come into existence. He spoke, and things happened immediately (Psalm 33:6–9).

4. The order of creation in Genesis 1 contradicts the order of events in the evolution story in at least 30 points. For example, the Bible says the earth was created before the sun and stars, just the opposite of

the big bang theory. The Bible says that fruit trees were created before any sea creatures and that birds were created before dinosaurs (which were made on Day 6, since they are land animals), exactly the opposite of the evolution story. The Bible says the earth was covered completely with water before dry land appeared, and then it was covered again at the Flood. Evolution theory says the earth has never been covered with a global ocean, and dry land existed before the first seas.

5. Exodus 20:8–11 resists all attempts to add millions of years anywhere in or before Genesis 1 because Exodus 20:11 says that God created everything in six days. The day-age view is ruled out because the plural form of the Hebrew word for day (yôm) is used in both parts of the commandment. The days of the Jewish work-week are the same as the days of Creation Week. God could have used several other words or phrases, here or in Genesis 1, if He meant to say "work six days because I created in six long, indefinite periods." But He didn't. These verses also rule out the gap theory or any attempt to add millions of years before Genesis 1:1 because God says He created the heavens, the earth, the sea, and all that is in them during the six days described in Genesis 1. He made nothing before those six days. It should also be noted that the fourth commandment is one of only a few of the Ten Commandments that contains a reason for the commandment. If God created over millions of years, He could have not given a reason for Sabbath-keeping or He could have given a theological or redemptive reason as He did elsewhere.

6. In Jesus' comments about Adam and Eve, Cain and Abel, Noah and the Flood, Sodom and Gomorrah, etc., He clearly took the events recorded in Genesis

as literal history, just as did all the New Testament writers. Several passages show that Jesus believed that man was created at the beginning of creation, not billions of years after the beginning (as all old-earth views imply), which confirms the young-earth creationist view (Mark 10:6 and 13:19 and Luke 11:50–51).10 His miracles also confirm the young-earth view. From His first miracle of turning water into wine (which revealed his glory as the Creator, cf. John 2:11 and John 1:1–5) to all His other miracles (e.g., Matthew 8:23–27, Mark 1:40–42), His spoken word brought an immediate, instantaneous result, just as God's word did in Creation Week.

7. The Bible teaches that there was no animal or human death before the Fall of Adam and Eve. So the geological record of rock layers and fossils could not have been millions of years before the Fall. See my development of this point below.

8. The nature of God as revealed in Scripture rules out the idea that He created over millions of years. See below.

9. The global catastrophic Flood of Noah was responsible for producing most (but not all) of the geological record of rock layers and fossils. Both a casual reading and careful exegesis show that this was not a local flood in Mesopotamia. It is most unreasonable to believe in a global, year-long Flood that left no geological evidence (or that it only left evidence in the low lands of the Fertile Crescent, as some suppose). The global evidence of sedimentary rock layers filled with land and marine fossils is exactly the kind of evidence we would expect from Noah's Flood. If most of the rock record is the evidence of the Flood, then there really is no geological evidence for millions of years. But the secular geologists deny the global Flood of Noah's

day because they deny that there is any geological evidence for such a flood. So, the fossiliferous rock record is either the evidence of Noah's Flood or the evidence of millions of years of geological change. It cannot be evidence of both. If we do not accept the geological establishment's view of Noah's Flood, then we cannot accept their view of the age of the earth. So, it is logically inconsistent to believe in both a global Noachian Flood and millions of years.

10. The genealogies of Genesis 5 and 11 give us the years from Adam to Abraham, who virtually all scholars agree lived about 2000 BC. This sets the date of creation at approximately 6,000+ years ago. Some young-earth creationists say the creation may be 10,000–12,000 years old. There are some biblical genealogies that do have names omitted (e.g., Matthew 1:1–17 or Mark 10:47). *[This is part of the reason why the late Henry Morris who is often times thought of as the "Father" of the creationist movement allowed a creation as early as 10,000 BC.]

11. For eighteen centuries the almost universal belief of the Church was that the creation began [4,000–5,500] years before Christ. So, young-earth creationism is historic Christian orthodoxy. It was also Jewish orthodoxy at least up to the end of the first century of church history. In light of this fact, it seems inconsistent with the truth-loving nature of God revealed in Scripture to think that for about 3,000 years God let faithful Jews and Christians (especially the writers of Scripture) believe that Genesis teaches a literal six-day creation about [6,000–7,500] years ago but that in the early nineteenth century He used godless men (scientists who rejected the Bible as God's inerrant Word) to correct the Church's understanding of Genesis.

Conclusion

The Bible clearly teaches a recent creation view in Genesis 1–11. That was the almost universal belief of the church for 1800 years. Progressive Creationism and Theistic Evolutionism in all their various forms (day-age view, gap theory, framework hypothesis, analogical days view, local flood view, etc.) are recent and novel interpretations that will not stand up to scrutiny with an open Bible. A growing body of overwhelming scientific evidence also shows that evolution and millions of years are religiously motivated myths masquerading as scientific fact.

Furthermore, the literal history of Genesis 1-11 is absolutely foundational to the truth of the rest of the Bible and the gospel itself. Taking these early chapters of Genesis in any other way undermines God's Word and the gospel of Jesus Christ, and over the past 200 years such compromises with evolution and millions of years have done incalculable damage to the spiritual health and evangelistic and missionary efforts of the Church. That compromise is one of the greatest reasons, if not the greatest reason, that Western Europe is now labeled "post-Christian" and Britain and America are rapidly approaching that spiritual state. Ultimately, the question of the age of the earth is a question of the truth and authority of Scripture. That's why the age of the earth matters so much and why the church cannot compromise with millions of years (or evolution). (https://answersingenesis.org/creationism/young-earth/young-earth-creationist-view-summarized-and-defended/)

Glossary

As a general courtesy it is important to define a few terms as general etiquette in their most short-forms.[1]

a priori – Known to be true independently of or in advance of experience of the subject matter; requiring no evidence for its validation or support

(] hoc – Lacking generality or justification (e.g., an AD hoc decision, an AD hoc committee)

agnosticism – A person who claims, with respect to any particular question, that the answer cannot be known with certainty

atheism – The doctrine or belief that there is no God

deism – The belief in the existence of a God on the evidence of reason and nature only, with rejection of supernatural revelation (distinguished from theism); belief in a God who created the world but has since remained indifferent to it

epistemology – A branch of philosophy that investigates the origin, nature, methods, and limits of human knowledge

history – The branch of knowledge dealing with past events

logic – The system or principles of reasoning applicable to any branch of knowledge or study

materialism – The philosophical theory that regards matter and its motions as constituting the universe, and all phenomena, including those of mind, as due to material agencies

metaphysics – The branch of philosophy that treats of first principles, includes ontology and cosmology, and is intimately

---

1   http://dictionary.reference.com.

connected with epistemology (literally meaning "beyond" normal physics)

naturalism – The view of the world that takes account only of natural elements and forces, excluding the supernatural or spiritual; the belief that all phenomena are covered by laws of science and that all teleological explanations are therefore without value

ontology – The branch of metaphysics that studies the nature of existence or being as such

origin science – The branch of "science" dealing with past unrepeatable events

philosophy – The rational investigation of the truths and principles of being, knowledge, or conduct

physicalism – The doctrine that all phenomena can be described in terms of space and time and that all meaningful statements are either analytic, as in logic and mathematics, or can be reduced to empirically verifiable assertions

positivism – A philosophical system founded by Auguste Comte, concerned with positive facts and phenomena, and excluding speculation upon ultimate causes or origins (e.g., talk of "God" is utterly meaningless)

scientism – The belief that the assumptions, methods of research, etc., of the physical and biological sciences are equally appropriate and essential to all other disciplines, including the humanities and the social sciences

theism – The belief in one God as the creator and ruler of the universe, without rejection of revelation (distinguished from deism)

Bibliography

Answers in Genesis. "Answers in Genesis." Accessed May 25, 2015. https://answersingenesis.org/.

"Bible History Online Images and Resources for Biblical History." Bible History Online Images and Resources for Biblical History. Accessed May 24, 2012. http://www.bible-history.com/.

Budge, E. A. Wallis. *The Gods of the Egyptians: Or, Studies in Egyptian Mythology*. New York: Dover Publications, 1969.

Cabal, Ted, Chad Brand, Paul Copan, and James Porter Moreland. *The Apologetics Study Bible: Understand Why You Believe*. Nashville, TN: Holman Bible Pub., 2007.

Cooper, Bill. *After the Flood: The Early Post-flood History of Europe*. Chichester: New Wine Press, 1995.

Copleston, Frederick C. *On the History of Philosophy and Other Essays*. London: Search Press, 1979.

Craig, William L. "ReasonableFaith.org—Defend Biblical Christianity, Apologetics, Bible Questions | Reasonable Faith." ReasonableFaith.org. Accessed May 25, 2012. http://www.reasonablefaith.org/.

Craig, William Lane. *Reasonable Faith: Christian Truth and Apologetics*. Wheaton, IL: Crossway Books, 1994.

Gee, Henry. *The Accidental Species: Misunderstandings of Human Evolution*. University of Chicago Press, 2015.

Geisler, Norman L. and Frank Turek. *I Don't Have Enough Faith to Be an Atheist*. Wheaton, IL: Crossway Books, 2004.

Grossman, Maxine L. *Rediscovering the Dead Sea Scrolls: An Assessment of Old and New Approaches and Methods*. Grand Rapids, MI: William B. Eerdmans Pub., 2010.

Grudem, Wayne A. *Systematic Theology: An Introduction to Biblical Doctrine.* Leicester, England: Inter-Varsity Press, 1994.

House, H. Wayne. *Intelligent Design 101: Leading Experts Explain the Key Issues.* Grand Rapids, MI: Kregel Publications, 2008.

Jastrow, Robert. *God and the Astronomers.* New York: Norton, 1978.

Kang, C. H., and Ethel R. Nelson. *The Discovery of Genesis: How the Truths of Genesis Were Found Hidden in the Chinese Language.* St. Louis: Concordia Pub. House, 1979.

Keller, Werner. *The Bible as History: A Confirmation of the Book of Books.* New York: W. Morrow, 1956.

Landis, Don. *The Genius of Ancient Man: Evolution's Nightmare.* Green Forest, AR: Master Books, 2012.

Laozi, Gia-fu Feng, and Jane English. *Tao Te Ching.* New York: Vintage Books, 1972.

McDowell, Josh. *The New Evidence That Demands a Verdict.* Nashville, TN: T. Nelson, 1999.

Meyer, Stephen C. *Signature in the Cell: DNA and the Evidence for Intelligent Design.* New York: HarperOne, 2009.

Montgomery, John Warwick. *History, Law and Christianity.* Edmonton, Alta.: Canadian Institute for Law, Theology & Public Policy, 2002.

Morris, Henry M., and J. Gordon. Henry. *The Henry Morris Study Bible: King James Version.* Green Forest, AR: Master Books, 2012.

Morris, Henry M. *The Genesis Record: A Scientific and Devotional Commentary on the Book of Beginnings.* Grand Rapids: Baker Book House, 1976.

Nagel, Thomas. *Mind and Cosmos: Why the Materialist Neo-Darwinian Conception of Nature Is Almost Certainly False.* New York: Oxford University Press, 2012.

Nelson, Ethel R., Richard E. Broadberry, and Ginger Tong. Chock. *God's Promise to the Chinese.* Dunlap, TN: Read Books Publisher, 1997.

Pandit, Subodh K. *Cross Examination: The Evidence for Belief.* Campus Press, 2011. doi:www.SearchSeminars.org.

Philosophia Christi. California: Evangelical Philosophical Society, 2001.

Plantinga, Alvin. *Where the Conflict Really Lies: Science, Religion, and Naturalism.* New York: Oxford University Press, 2011.

Price, Randall. *Searching for the Original Bible.* Eugene, Or.: Harvest House Publishers, 2007.

Price, Randall. *The Stones Cry Out.* Eugene, Or.: Harvest House Publishers, 1997.

Rosenberg, Alexander. *The Atheist's Guide to Reality: Enjoying Life without Illusions.* New York: W.W. Norton, 2011.

Sherwin-White, A. N. *Roman Society and Roman Law in the New Testament.* Oxford: Clarendon Press, 1963.

Slick, Matt. "CARM–The Christian Apologetics & Research Ministry." CARM–The Christian Apologetics & Research Ministry. Accessed May 24, 2012. https://carm.org.

Stroud, James E. *Mere Christian Apologetitcs.* Xulon, 2011.

Stroud, James E. *The Philosophy of History Naturalism and Religion; a Historiographical Approach to Origins.* Tate Pub & Enterprises Llc, 2013.

Wells, Jonathan. *Icons of Evolution: Science or Myth?: Why Much of What We Teach about Evolution Is Wrong.* Washington, DC: Regnery Pub., 2000.

Wikipedia: The Free Encyclopedia. San Francisco: Wikimedia Foundation. http://en.wikipedia.org/.

Wright, N. T. *The Resurrection of the Son of God.* Fortress Press, 2003.

Wurmbrand, Richard. *The Answer to the Atheist's Handbook.* Bartlesville, OK: Living Sacrifice Books, 1993.

Zacharias, Ravi K. *Can Man Live without God.* Dallas: Word Pub., 1994.

Zondervan. KJV *Archaeological Study Bible: An Illustrated Walk through Biblical History and Culture.* Grand Rapids, MI: Zondervan, 2010.

About the Author

James Stroud has an MA in ancient and classical history and a BA in philosophy of religion. He is also a member of the Society of Collegiate Scholars, the Association of Ancient Historians (AAH), Society for Historical Archaeology (SHA), and the Philosophical Research Society (PRS), and he has personally visited many of the historic sites referenced in this book. James recently returned to the Midwest from the New York City area, where he and his wife, Gina, lived in 2009–2012. They are currently working on opening a small Philosophy of History museum and cultural center in partnership with the Great Passion Play. (See www.NWABibleMuseum.org and www.TheLollards.org for more information.)

Made in the USA
Columbia, SC
16 June 2018